WALK ME THROUGH YOUR RESUME

essays

MARTHA COONEY

For Bill and Pat Cooney, the greatest parents in the world

Contents

Microwaving in the Ivy League

WHEN I WENT TO COLLEGE at the University of Pennsylvania, the Penn kids and I did not understand each other. They didn't know what a beef 'n' beer was. I didn't know what they meant when they talked about "unpaid internships."

Where I grew up in northeast Philly, the uniform was simple. Clothing was dictated by season. Eagles shirt in the fall, Phillies shirt in the spring, and your best jersey for church on Sunday. Add gray sweatpants and a necklace with your name spelled out in fake gold and you were good.

At Penn, jewelry wasn't fake, and sweatpants were only for kids headed to lacrosse practice. There were lots of shirts that said *Patagonia*. I was afraid to ask what that was. Was it the name of a country? Were these souvenir shirts equivalent to the knockoff *I Love NY* shirt I bought on Canal Street last year? How was it possible that *all* these students had been to Patagonia on vacation?

Guys wore pants with small animals on them: turtles, whales, dogs, flamingos. They topped them with pastel polo shirts. I was mortified for them, but the confusing part was, these dudes walked with a swagger. I didn't know what was real anymore. I resisted a continual urge to grab them by the shoulders and shake them, warning them that if they walked off campus into Philadelphia they would get their ass kicked.

The food was different too. For the first time in my life, I heard people say that pasta was not healthy. In the dining hall, girls didn't go back for seconds. They looked at me blankly when I reminded them they could go ahead, it's all you can eat.

My freshman hall was populated with characters. One of the gems was my next-door neighbor John, a wholesome square with a dry wit and a heart of gold.

John was straight out of a J.D. Salinger novel—a prep school Catholic who drank whole milk by the glass. He pinned the flag of Maryland to his dorm room wall, and when temperatures rose, he snapped up his purple high school letterman's jacket. John "did crew." This meant he got up early to row a boat on the Schuylkill River with a bunch of other guys while another guy yelled at them from a separate boat telling them which way to turn. I don't know. Seems like the system could be improved.

John was very quiet. The rest of our group was a loud gang of keyed-up eighteen-year-olds trying to out-clown each other, and John was the dad of the pack. He watched the pranking with a pensive face, occasionally recording on his Panasonic camcorder. Although he didn't say much, John had a steady confidence; a satisfying type of person to have around. While the rest of us roasted each other constantly, John paced himself with well-timed zingers that were the most on point due to so much time observing.

Because he was so unshakable, we loved trying to provoke him. On April Fool's Day, his roommate switched their two halves of the room, measuring things to the centimeter so everything on the walls would be a bizarro-world mirror image when John walked in after crew practice. John took it in slowly, nodded and said, "Well." Getting a rise out of him was a real win. Whenever he was frustrated with me, he'd sputter, "God bless it, Martha!"

During the summers, when I worked at overnight camp, John sent handwritten letters ("even though stamps are 37 cents now – give me a break.") He didn't get drunk until junior year, when he threw up over the arm of our living room couch during a party.

After freshman year, a bunch of us from the hall moved to a high-rise apartment dorm. Four of us girls shared three bedrooms, and John and his roommate lived next door. We were on the seventh floor of a twenty-four story building, with a living room overlooking four frat houses. Being seven floors up was high enough for me. I had an intense fear of heights, especially if I was near open windows in high places; what if I lost control of my senses and decided to bust through the screen and jump out? So I never opened any of the windows or stood near them if I could help it.

I felt like I lived in a luxurious hotel. We had a black-and-white theme in the living room, with posters of James Dean, Marilyn Monroe, and *The Godfather*. We had a VCR/DVD combo player. My roommates had brought an ice cream maker, sandwich griller, espresso machine, and microwave.

We didn't have a microwave growing up. My Italian mother found the idea sacrilegious. "I cook from scratch! I use a pot!" she liked to say. "Those things give off laser beams!" (She did eventually get a microwave, but for years she unplugged it between uses.)

Having the microwave in the apartment opened a whole new world to me. I watched with fascination as my roommate Jen used it to cook bacon. Incredible! Every week I experimented with a new microwavable option. One week I bought a bag of frozen SuperPretzel soft pretzels, like the ones we used to get from the hot display case on the boardwalk down the shore. I looked forward to making a pretzel in the microwave for the first time.

It was a bitter night in December, the last night of finals week. Jen and I were in the apartment, putting off studying, and our other roommates were out. There was a knock at the door. "John, you don't have to knock!" Jen said when she opened it. "Just come in!"

"A gentleman always knocks," John said. He sat down on the cow print elastic-covered futon. The three of us debated walking to the library to get work done, but decided it was way too cold.

3

"I'm going to the rooftop lounge to outline all my Poli Sci reading before the exam tomorrow." Jen rose to get her backpack. "If anyone interrupts me, I will be very angry."

John had to study for "MacroEcon," whatever that was, and I had to write a paper. Everyone dispersed. It was rare to be alone in the apartment, so instead of working in my room, I spread out at our little dining table. The string of red chili pepper lights blinked above me. At 11:30 pm I remembered the SuperPretzels.

I pulled the bag from the freezer and carefully wet the top of a pretzel, as directed, to apply the salt crystals. I put the pretzel in the microwave, glanced at the bag, saw the 3, set the timer for three minutes, and pushed the button. Just enough time to listen all the way through to Mariah Carey's *All I Want for Christmas is You*.

Mariah was hitting a "Youuuuuuuu" and I was stabbing the air above me with my pointer finger when I noticed a burning smell.

The microwave beeped. I pushed the button to open it, and a rush of black smoke poured into the room. It was like a bomb had dropped. Through the haze inside the microwave, I barely made out a melted, charred black lump of pretzel. I grabbed the bag, blinking stinging eyes at the directions. *Heat for 30 seconds.* Thirty seconds. Not three minutes! Why, why, why didn't I have the common cultural knowledge of how long a pretzel should be cooked in a microwave?! That space in my brain was probably taken up by the schedule for the 67 SEPTA bus.

The room was so thick with smoke now that I couldn't breathe. *Smoke inhalation is a thing. This is a situation.* I ran over to the windows to open them, but one glance down seven stories and I backed away. I couldn't bring myself to do it. I ran back to the microwave through the smoke. I went back to the window. I went back to the microwave.

There was a knock at the door.

I flung it open. There was John, a polo-shirt-clad Oliver Twist holding a bowl of dry Cinnamon Toast Crunch. "Martha. Do you have any milk? I drank all of—What is going on?" Smoke billowed behind my head and surged out of the apartment into the hallway. John stood with his mouth slightly open, looking at me with the expression of a father who finds his child on the bathroom floor, having discovered scissors and cut off all her hair.

"Come in! I need to close the door!" I said. The black cloud of smoke was filling up the corridor. "Before the—"

The fire alarm in the hallway went off.

"I'm not going in there!" John said. He was still holding his cereal bowl with two hands. "Martha, you need to get out of there!"

The alarm screamed and flashed. Doors started opening and heads poked out. Eric, our RA, ran hysterically out of his apartment, exhilarated to assume his post after a dormant semester of self-sufficient sophomore residents ignoring his invitations to "let me know if you need anything." He ran up and down the hall, banging doors and yelling importantly in his best FEMA voice.

I had to stop this. It was midnight on the last night of finals. The 796 other residents of this building were either sleeping because their morning exam would determine if their grades were good enough for med school, or, if they did things more my speed, they were cramming a semester's worth of unattended History of Ancient Greece class material into a three-hour study block fueled only by Mountain Dew Code Red. Nobody had time for this right now.

People were already streaming for the exits. The elevators had shut down in automatic response to the alarm, and as someone opened the door to the stairwell, I saw a stampede of bodies galloping down the stairs. The building was being evacuated.

Shit.

If there was one thing I had learned about Penn kids by now, it was that they did not love to be inconvenienced.

I started running, before things got ugly. Down seven flights and into the lobby, straight to the front desk where two student staffers appeared less than confident. I leaned over the desk and spoke in a whisper. "It was me," I said. "I set off the alarm. There's no fire. It's fine. You can turn it off."

The boy blinked and pointed to the front door. Multiple fire engines flashing in front of the building were parked at opposing angles, ready for a standoff. Guys on the truck unwound a hose. Firefighters pushed their way in through the revolving door and headed for where I was standing at the desk.

I looked the other way. Waves of students poured into the lobby from both stairwells and rolled out the front doors under security's direction. It was an enraged mob of type A's who had just descended twenty-four flights to stand outside in eighteen degrees in their underwear and pajamas. Each was angrier than the last, ready to kill the idiot who'd set off the fire alarm.

This would cement my legacy, and not in a good way. They wouldn't forget something like this. These kids were currently living page 125 of their autobiography and this interruption was not in the plan. Who knew what they were capable of at this hour, hopped up on caffeine and Adderall? My body would be found at the bottom of the library steps, Sharpied up and covered in sticky notes, each one bearing the name of a victim who had to retake Statistics after having their all-nighter disrupted. I wondered in passing if the Ivy League had a witness protection program.

I was out of time to make a plan. The firemen were talking to the front desk guy, and the front desk guy was pointing to me. Head lowered, I gave the firefighters the apartment number, then went back to the stairs, swimming upstream against the risk takers who were last to leave. At the seventh-floor stairwell, I stood facing the cinder block wall, hands in the pockets of my gray sweatpants, and hid. I couldn't face it. I didn't know how to use a microwave, I was afraid of open windows in high places, and I still didn't know where or what Patagonia was.

The alarm stopped. Within minutes, the horde was stamping past me back up the stairs. I stayed in my corner, trying to look casual.

I waited until the corridors emptied, then opened the heavy stairwell door and returned to our apartment. Two firemen were in the living room with Jen and John. The room still had a gauzy curtain of smoke, but the windows were open, and freezing gusts of air came in through the screen. Everyone looked at me.

I raised my hand meekly to the firefighters. "Hey, uh, I was the one that did it."

"Yeah, we got it," one of them said. "Just leave the windows open for a while."

They left.

"Don't worry," Jen said. "We already instant messaged everybody and told them it was you."

I didn't want to make another pretzel in front of everyone, so I waited until the next day. It worked out fine.

John has two kids now. He hasn't changed at all. When I was visiting his family and Sullivan, the six-year-old, farted in my face, John slapped his knee and said, "God bless it, Sullivan!" He still drinks milk by the glass.

This is What Happens When You Lie to the Irish

I WAS LIVING IN BELFAST, Northern Ireland on a six-month tourist visa, working under the table as a nanny. I made enough cash in hand to rent a room on a street called Ava Gardens and go out to the pubs on the weekends. It was a good time.

I loved the Irish. My accent was a conversation starter, and everyone was friendly. Bus drivers acted personally delighted for me to join them. When I dumped about fifty small coins into the fare box the driver laughed and said, "Ach, were ye up all night countin' that?" If I pulled that in Philly someone would push me down the steps while the bus drove away. The last time I took the subway in New York, a stranger sat down next to me, smiled, and exposed himself. Belfast passengers lined up in a civilized manner and thanked the driver. Delightful.

My six month stay started winding down, and I was unhappy about it. I didn't want to leave. Spring in Belfast was so beautiful. The days were long and pink light fell over the brick terraced houses in the evening. My friend Lisa and I had just chipped in to buy the entire *Sex and the City* box set and we were working our way through it. I'd recently joined a coed tag rugby team and not to brag, but I was a natural. I would go home to Ava Gardens, sit on the edge of the bathtub with my legs covered in dirt, and think about how satisfied I was with life at that moment.

I'd also started seeing this Irish guy, Ryan McConnell. He was a ginger from County Cavan, and his accent was particularly musical and enchanting. His stories of growing up in the countryside sounded like old documentaries watched on VHS after your teacher rolled in the audio-visual cart. "We had this row of trees going all the way down the lane, and we would climb from tree to tree to tree to tree," he told me as my pupils dilated. One night, after riding bicycles back over the bridge to my house from a pub quiz, I told Ryan McConnell about my scheme to stay in Belfast past my visa.

Northern Ireland is technically part of the United Kingdom, even though it's on the island of Ireland, and shares a border with the Republic. (For more information, please see *Derry Girls*.) This was post-peace agreement and pre-Brexit, and you could drive back and forth over the border without showing your passport or stating your business.

So, if I left Belfast by plane and flew into Dublin in Ireland, I could get my passport stamped by Dublin immigration and take a bus over the border into Belfast with no immigration checks and the official record stating I was in Ireland. I could then organize another decoy flight to "return" to Belfast from Dublin after the required three months away. (Was it wrong to be pleased with a silver lining of centuries of political strife? I had done my part for the peace process; I was a Catholic with Protestant friends. I'd earned this!)

Ryan McConnell listened to my idea. He said, "Ach, Marta. Don't fly into Dublin. There's too much immigration security. It'll be crawlin' wit' police. I tell you what to do. You want to fly into Knock airport. Knock, in the west of Ireland, it's a wee little airport. You'll walk right through; they won't even look twice at you."

In the accent, his plan sounded flawless. I said, great idea. I'll go to Knock.

The cheapest plane ticket to Knock took me through East Midlands airport in England, halfway between Nottingham (Robin Hood!) and Leicester (cheese?). I booked the flight for the day before my six-month stay was up and got on the plane with my laptop bag and a book. I was impressed with myself for figuring out the plan; I'd be back at Ava Gardens in time for dinner.

The plane landed in a windy rain. I walked down the rickety steps and into Knock airport, an empty room smaller than my high school gym. There were two lines: European passports or non-European passports. No one else from my plane got into the second line. I walked forward.

The immigration officer, a beefy man with dark hair and blue eyes, did not look like someone who watched videos for advice on practicing a power pose or overcoming imposter syndrome in the workplace. He looked at my passport, then looked at me.

Our eyes met. I knew, and I knew that he knew, and I knew that he knew that I knew, that I was fucked.

"Where are you going?" he started. "Where are you coming from? What's your business here? What do you do for a living? If you're traveling all over Ireland, why haven't you got a bigger bag?"

I recited my lies, but perhaps not with the confidence required. Then he asked, "How much money do you have?" It was a dirty move.

"Who are you staying with in Dublin?" he asked.

This was the first positive sign. I pulled out a piece of paper with my Dubliner friend Kelsey's phone number and address. Now he would copy it down and wave me through, like they always did. I'd flown into Dublin many times and they never called the number. I had used Kelsey's real information for authenticity, but I hadn't given her a heads up about the scheme because I was so sure that they wouldn't bother to call.

"Wait here," the officer said. He took the piece of paper and went over to a glass booth with a telephone. Kelsey told me later the mystery caller growled "Are you expecting any visitors?" when she picked up. Caught off guard, she said "What? No." He hung up.

The officer came back out and looked into my eyes again. "She's not expecting you," he said. "That's deception. Go stand against the wall, you're getting back on the plane you came on."

I tend to be a planner, so I said, "What's going to happen when I get off that plane?"

He said, "I don't know, they'll probably deport you. It's not my concern, I'm not letting you in. Go stand against the wall."

I went and stood against the wall in a stupor. *Deception.* A breach of the sacred trust I'd once shared with the country I loved. Could I go back and deliver a speech? *Hold on, you don't understand, I don't mean any harm. You guys know me! I'm a big fan! Let me sing you all the lyrics to "Whiskey in the Jar." Please!*

How could they reject me? After all the positive word of mouth I'd spread about this place! During a recent karaoke night I had even put a donation in the collection hat "for the Republican movement."

As the reality of the situation dawned on me, I felt like kicking myself. How could I have been led so astray by a magical redhead? Everybody knows if you're going to execute a scheme, you have to plan for all eventualities. Why did I expect it to be so easy? *"Oh, hello boys! Just breezing through!"* The officer really had me with the bag thing. I could tell that even if he had let me through immigration, he would have gotten me somehow. I'd have gone to buy my bus ticket and said, "One way to Belfast, please," and he would've popped up in the window wearing a green eyeshade, rubbing his hands together. "Thought you said you were going to Dublin! FOILED!"

Still standing against the wall, the beefy officer eyeing me from his station, I was getting more and more scared when a flight landed. Fifty white-haired elders shuffled by, clutching rosary beads and looking over at me with concern. I suddenly remembered. Knock was the site of a holy shrine that attracted pilgrims from around the world. It was the only reason anyone ever traveled to Knock. It was the only reason they had an airport. I stared straight ahead as the parade of believers passed by, mumbling to each other, "What's she done?" and shaking their heads at the shame of it. Sin! Lies! *DECEPTION!*

My officer personally escorted me to my plane and to an aisle seat in the middle section. He pointed to me as he spoke with the flight attendant, and I looked away, focusing on the buttons of my red pea coat. I looked way too mousy for what was going down right now. It was embarrassing. If I had known everyone was going to be thinking I was a mysterious international criminal, I would have done something with my hair. I could have found a trench coat with a fur collar at a secondhand store. Maybe some leather gloves.

The whole way back to East Midlands, I leaned forward in my seat, a sinking feeling in my stomach, preparing myself for the jail cell. It would probably be cold. I can't sleep when it's cold, and that would throw off the whole next day. I assumed I would get a sandwich. But they put mayonnaise on all their sandwiches there, and I hate mayonnaise. So I wouldn't be able to eat the sandwich. What if they rationed toilet paper? I was sure it wouldn't be enough.

The plane landed, and as I approached the front of the line, I saw why it had been crawling so slowly. There was an officer checking everyone's passport against a printout of my photo. No point making him work any harder. I volunteered, "It's me," as if claiming a raffle prize. He took me out of the line and delivered me to an interrogation room. A new officer sat on one side of the desk, and I sat down on the other side. How was I going to play this? *"Bless me Father for I have sinned"* … or *"let me walk you through my resume"*?

This officer was quite young and seemed to be thinking hard about how to proceed. *I know, right?* I wanted to say. *I don't want to be here … you don't want to be here … let's just call it.* He started asking questions. To be honest, he was really nice. He asked about my work, my finances, my future plans. It was basically a date.

I admitted I had been planning to return to Belfast. The gentleman officer considered everything and told me I had to leave by tomorrow. "We'll be alerting the authorities in Belfast, and if you don't leave within twenty-four hours, they'll deport you," he said, but not unkindly. Relieved, I assured him I would sort out a flight and leave the next day. He wrote down his name and phone number and said that I should call him once my flight information was confirmed. Maybe so they could close the case—or was it so we could keep in touch?

I got back to Belfast, called all my friends, and packed up my things. Ryan McConnell said, "Ach, Marta! I feel terrible! It's my fault. I'm the one who told you to go to Knock; it's my fault. Marta, I'm so sorry!" My jaw went slack and all the resentment left me. No, I said. I wasn't worthy of the scheme. It was my time to go.

When I got back to the States, I called the gentleman officer with my flight information and left a voicemail. It's been quite a few years. I haven't heard back.

How to Deliver Phone Books

GATHER ROUND, CHILDREN, AND I will tell you about a thing we used to have called the Phone Book.

It was a majestic object. You could find the address of any crush or the phone number of any prank call victim for the low entry fee of knowing their father's full name. You could give a short kid a boost at the dinner table or flatten a rolled-up art project.

For your fingers to do the walking through this informational jamboree, it had to be delivered by a human person. I took up the honored position in the final days of the phone book era.

Seattle and San Francisco had just banned the books for being wasteful and useless in the digital age, but in Philadelphia, they were still hanging on. The world was changing, children, and I was lucky enough to sneak under the velvet drape and stand in the back before the big show ended. Travel with me, back to 2011. You're just a kid, with stars in your eyes.

Delivering Phone Books: A How-To Guide

GET A CAR

Turn 28. Move back in with your parents. Have your dad teach you to drive in the Toys 'R' Us parking lot. Take your driving exam. You don't need to remember what hazard lights are—the instructor will let it slide. Get that plastic Golden Ticket in your grasp and accept your parents' hand-me-down '96 Saturn with an appreciative hat tip. You're on your way.

PLAN YOUR FINANCES

Hole up in your childhood bedroom. Stare at a pad of chart paper unearthed from 1997 and figure out how to pay your bills. Tell yourself you can be a successful freelance artist if you supplement by living like Kramer from _Seinfeld_. He gets by on schemes; so can you. All it takes is a little financial planning.

List ideas to make money. _Bring penny jar to Coinstar. Post_ Breakfast at Tiffany's _DVD on eBay. Sell eggs?_ Consider the state of your ovarian jewels. Would you? Could you? Would they even want them? You spoke with a lazy "S" as a child. Anyway, you're too old. You should have thought of this during college before your cash crop frittered itself away. Instead, you ignored the financial advice enunciated into the microphone by the drip from Career Services at that senior year presentation and hovered at the free pizza table in back, quietly wrapping takeaway slices in a napkin.

SEARCH CRAIGSLIST

Embrace 2011 Craigslist gig postings as the glossy, light-drenched Pinterest vision board they are. It's a paint chip catalog for life, and you can swirl your brush in any can. You can work on a moving crew (create choreographed assembly line dance for truck load-up; cargo shorts). You can count pedestrians on the street for a foot traffic study (pep up intersection with jokey pick-me-ups for passersby; neon hat). You can hand-address a stranger's wedding invitations in elegant penmanship (lay desk with candles and white flowers; maxi skirt).

The ad for the phone book delivery gig is the opportunity you've been searching for. The job requires a car. You have a car. You can be a professional driver.

VISUALIZE YOUR FUTURE

Envision your life as a professional driver. You'll make your own hours, and no manager will be hanging over your shoulder. Just you and the open road, listening to the radio. After a day's work, you'll stop at the diner and have pie and coffee at the counter. You can sit at the counter without hesitation because you'll basically be a trucker—one of the guys. What kind of pie do truckers eat? Is meringue too unsubstantial? More like cherry, right? Will they provide you with a CB radio? What about a course in lingo? "Ten-four" was standard school bus driver conversation, but what if that was code for drugs? You'll embarrass yourself if you say the wrong thing. Look this up.

Call the number in the listing and write down the time to show up for training. It's not an interview. They'll take anybody.

DRESS FOR SUCCESS

Choose your orientation outfit carefully. It's at the warehouse on State Road under 95 in the Northeast, between the prison and Sweet Lucy's BBQ. Don't wear your Penn t-shirt—do you want to look like an asshole? Don't be too girly, either. Your Mike Schmidt green Phillies tee with the shamrock that you got at Irish Weekend in Wildwood is appropriate.

LEARN YOUR TRADE

Sit in a folding chair with ten other applicants in the cavernous warehouse full of wooden pallets stacked with shrink-wrapped yellow phone books. Fill out paperwork. Watch a DVD on good customer service. Carol, your fearless leader, will press stop on the DVD and say, "I'm telling you now, do not throw my books. People like to throw the books; think they're saving time. Then I get a call, what happened to my phone book?" Relish the richness of her smoker's voice and sit up straight like a good student. You won't throw books. You'll nestle them gently by the front door like robin's eggs.

Bounce along the gravel of Carol's voice and learn about the GPS tracker you'll wear on a lanyard. "It monitors your movements to make sure you go up to every single door on your route. If there's a vicious dog or a good reason you can't leave a book at a house, mark it on your sheet." She stresses having a buddy join you on your route, so one person can drive and the other can hop in and out to deliver. "Otherwise it's too hard to keep starting and stopping."

Start to panic. No one warned you this was going to be like ballroom dancing or birthing class. You don't have a partner. Should you ask someone here to be your buddy? What if they laugh in your face? What if they insist on using their car, and you have to go with their choice of radio station? Commit to lonewolfdom, like Batman. At least, Batman before he paired up with Robin. You got into this field to enjoy your own company and listen to music of your choice throughout a relaxed workday. You're a professional driver.

Carol's voice is a wood-paneled room filled with rug-layered carpet and paintings of ducks. Close your eyes and travel to a nostalgic place while her words crackle warmly in the air. "Each book has to be bagged. I advise bagging as you go." Try not to let your disagreement show. You're going to do this your way. You're going to disrupt the phone book delivery system.

FANTASIZE ABOUT RUNNING NEXT YEAR'S TRAINING

Brainstorm name games for a group of ten. Include a human bingo ice-breaker to match up potential partners based on personality traits. Think about snacks. Dark chocolate bars broken into pieces. Vitamin Water. Bagels. Roleplay scenarios could liven things up a bit and prepare everyone for situations that could be encountered on the job.

You put a phone book on a front step and hear a couple arguing loudly behind their front door. What do you do?

Reflect on your skill set. Are you experienced in facilitation and conflict resolution? Knock on the door and offer to help. Better at vocal performance? Yell live commentary through the window. Having your own relationship troubles? You're too close to the issue. Move on.

You notice a suspicious character stealing the phone book you just delivered. Do you address it?

If a tree falls in the woods, are you responsible for its actions? This can stir up a good philosophical discussion. Brush up on Jean-Paul Sartre. If you have any visible tattoos that reflect a strong point of view, your argument better walk the walk.

An attractive man opens the door and invites you in for a glass of water. Do you accept?

Think this one through! On the one hand, personal safety. On the other, a great how-we-met story.

PREPARE YOUR EQUIPMENT

Once your TI-81 is hanging heavy around your neck and your route map is in hand, bring your car to the loading zone. Everyone else has a van, truck or sizable SUV that fits their entire route's worth of phone books. Your Saturn is too small to fit more than half your load. Try your best! Shove phone books under seats. Pile them on the dash. Tower them in the back seat to the point that your rearview mirror is useless. Don't be distracted by everyone watching you struggle. Your Saturn is scrappy and so are you! Carol will look at your orphaned phone books waiting on the pallet. "Just come back for the second half of your route," she says. (Sandpaper on toast. Delicious).

The Saturn will trundle along like Ichabod Crane's weighed-down, ribs-pokey horse (Disney version). Work out your plan for maximum efficiency. You'll bag the books first, then hit the route.

CONFRONT YOUR CRITICS

Argue with your mom as you bring piles of phone books into the house. You want to prop the door open. She wants to open and close the screen door as you go in and out ("There's bats"). Argue about the bagging process. She sides with Carol and says you should bag as you go. Tell her she and Carol are both wrong. Fill the living room with yellow. Free the book bundles from shrink wrap. Shove each book into its own orange plastic bag. The bags are the consistency of water. It's a fun whack-a-mole game to stack the bagged books as they slip 'n slide off the pile. Push books to the side so your dad can see the TV. "These better be out of here by tomorrow," your mom will say. She'll add, "I never should have given her that car." Great innovators have always had doubters. Pay no mind.

DRIVE WITH CONFIDENCE

Start the day fresh. Load the slippery pre-bagged books into your car. Retire your expectations of order and accept that the back seat is a Jell-O wrestling party. Look over your route and begin with enthusiasm. Carol said each route should take two days. Not for you, it won't. Embody the cockiness of an untrained Teach for America grad who decides they're the one the world needs to start a charter school. You'll knock this out in one shift.

On the first block, edge the car slowly down the street and keep it running as you walk up and down each driveway to drop the books. Isn't this using gas? Go back and move your car when people start beeping. Start the park-and-carry. Find a spot at the end of the block, load as many books as you can in your arms and make your way down the street like a reverse trick-or-treater. As you drop each book, you have to readjust your hold on the pile. Try instead to grip the plastic bags from the top. Go for five in each hand. Feel the plastic stretch out like Fruit Roll-Ups as the books dangle. You won't need to go to the gym anymore. What an ideal job.

KNOW YOUR VALUE

After two blocks of leaving books on doorsteps, realize you're getting the hang of it. This is what it's like to be a public servant! You're the milkman, the junk peddler of old, the door-to-door vacuum seller. You'll become a pillar of the community, making your rounds with news of the weather and gossip about the neighbor's knee injury. Word will travel when it's phone book delivery season, and neighbors will leave you fresh blueberry buckles covered with rooster-print towels. Or tokens crafted from last year's phone book pages, like a decoupage mason jar or birdcage, in honor of you and your noble profession. Think about how you can jazz up the occasion each year going forward, maybe with a costume or funny hat. You could turn the whole delivery process into a musical:

(Twirling and leaping as you drop each book)
"You can find anything in a phone book,
Someone to fix a pipe,
Someone to cobble a shoe,
You can find anything in the phone book,
It's all right here for youuuu!"

(Sitting down on curb, wistful)
"I can find anything in the phone book,
Someone to sell a car,
Someone to chop a tree,
I can find anything in the phone book,
(whisper) But how do I find meeee?"

(Wave to applause)

Mentally compose email to favorite college professor: you're having a breakthrough about that Urban Studies course. Here you are in the trenches, making an impact step by step, house by house. Providing the very ingredients of communication that make a city run. Hand a phone book to an older gentleman working in his garage. Nod as he thanks you. Head down the driveway, glance back with a satisfied smile, and watch him drop the book directly into his recycle bin.

KEEP YOUR SPIRITS UP

Times get tough on the road. It turns out you don't get to listen to the radio much, since most of your time is spent walking back and forth to houses. Live for the moments when you catch fifteen full seconds of a song on the drive to a new street. Know your limits: even though the pile in the back looks untouched, it feels like you've been delivering all day. Go home for dinner. "Are you leaving those phone books in the car?" your mom will ask. "Someone could break in. They might wanna sell them." You planned to knock out a whole route in one day, but it takes you three days to do half the load. Refill your car at the warehouse. Your old friends from orientation are loading up for their second route. Remember the tortoise and the hare.

Transition from happy Wells Fargo Wagon Girl (see: *The Music Man*) to snarling at dogs and avoiding eye contact with those who don't want to accept your offering. "I don't want this," a homeowner will say as you hold out their book. Tell them you must give it to them anyway. Tell yourself it's not giving up to start bagging as you go. You have the right to pivot based on data results. When the rain starts pouring, give yourself a break. You don't want to ruin the books. Carol wouldn't like it.

Take the phone books on field trips to the Dunkin' drive thru and to visit friends who are in town for the day. Let the books serve as seating as your 6'-3", 215-pound minor league ballplayer friend folds himself on top of the stacks in the front, while his tinier wife perches on the piles in back, her body touching the ceiling, when you give them a ride to their hotel. When you drive back to your route, roll down the window (there's no A/C in the Saturn). Watch the pile of orange plastic bags in the back seat blow apart, cyclone around the car, paper themselves to the ceiling, and whirl out the window. Roll up the window. People pay for sweat baths. You're burning calories.

Promise the books they'll get to their forever home soon, but in the meantime, they can meet new friends and hear bedtime stories as you toss Wawa sandwich wrappers into the back and play the Phillies broadcast on the radio. Finish the route under a drizzle.

SAY GOODBYE

Turn in your lanyard at the warehouse and tell them you won't be doing another route, since you got another job. It's not a lie; you're gathering Craigslist babysitting gigs like nuts in an apron. Carol won't fight you. She knew you weren't going to go far. She gave you a chance, though, because doesn't everyone deserve to try?

"Congratulations," Carol will say with sincerity. It's the last time you'll ever hear her voice. Savor it, like chewing a Sugar Daddy pop. The Saturn will feel much lighter on the drive home. Tomorrow, you can get back on Craigslist and apply to play a dead bride at a Halloween party. It pays seventy-five dollars.

Don't Snore at the Movies

YEARS AGO, DURING A CRAIGSLIST phase, I clicked on an ad titled "Ivy League Tutor for GRE." The listing was short. Twenty dollars an hour to help someone study for the graduate school entrance exam.

I had taken the GRE myself a few years ago, though I couldn't remember my scores and hadn't yet gone to grad school, but at that tax-free pay rate I sure could pretend to be an expert on how to study for it. I sent in my resume.

I met Rob the Tutee at a Borders bookstore cafe in the suburbs. He wore a tweed sports jacket with elbow patches and told me all the things we had in common based on my resume. Very good, very good, but let's get to the twenty dollars an hour. So we dove into studying for the GRE, meeting up three times a week to review vocab and work through practice tests.

He was an odd duck. Anti-social, maybe. He told me he made a habit of pulling out his phone and filming awkward encounters involving strangers. He showed me one video: he had taken someone's parking spot, and the guy came over to challenge him about it; saying nothing, Rob started filming the guy at close range as he raged in his face. This was the very beginning of the smartphone era; few people had video cameras on their phones, much less used them to film someone losing it over noncompliance in the Popeye's line.

One day we were reviewing some math when an older woman happened by our table. She introduced herself: his mother. They exchanged awkward hellos and she asked what we were up to. Rob was silent, so I said cheerfully, "We're doing some tutoring."

She said, "Who's tutoring who?"

I don't know why I felt some kind of loyalty to the Tutee, but I didn't want to blow his cover just in case he didn't want her to know, so I said, "We're kind of helping each other," which she found quite amusing and asked Rob if he would be home for dinner that night.

I was looking for additional gigs on Craigslist when I saw it. "Ivy League Tutor for GRE." Rob had posted his ad again, just two days ago. I emailed him immediately: "What is this? Am I being fired?" He remained evasive, but the next day when we were studying, it all came out. He was meeting up with another tutor today after me, and I needed to leave before she got there because she didn't know about me.

He was two-time tutoring.

I said, "You advertised for a tutor so you could meet girls."

He said, "Maybe."

I said, "Are you even taking the GRE?"

"Yeah," Rob said. "I just figured I would kill two birds with one stone."

I made it clear that we were not going to go in that direction, but I was willing to keep tutoring, because twenty dollars an hour ... is twenty dollars an hour. So we continued, and he continued to speed date other potential tutors, but it didn't interfere with our sessions. In fact, we were almost becoming friends. Is that what we were? We must have been, because a few nights after he took the GRE exam and our tutoring was over, I invited him to hang out. My friend Chrissy and her boyfriend Kyle and I planned to go see a movie, and the Tutee was going to come along.

It was a midnight movie at the Neshaminy AMC 24, at a mall outside of northeast Philly. The lobby was swarming with late night movie goers. The Tutee showed up wearing a Far Side t-shirt tucked into Levis with combat boots. The place was packed, not a seat empty. We sat in a row: Kyle on the end, Chrissy, then me, then Rob the Tutee.

The movie was *The Proposal* with Sandra Bullock and Ryan Reynolds. They work together and hate each other, but for green card reasons they need to fake an engagement, and hijinks ensue. Plus, Betty White.

About a third of the way into the story, loud snores erupted from the other side of the theater. We were right in the middle of the scene between Ryan and Sandra about her bird tattoo; it's a very key moment (you know it if you've seen it), and the crowd started rustling in response to the snoring guy, whose sounds were filling up the room. Rob looked around with a delighted smile on his face. After a couple minutes of snoring, a girl sitting two rows in front of us started yelling. "Yo! You're snoring! Wake up!" The snoring guy had what appeared to be his girlfriend next to him, and she nudged him awake. There was a merciful silence, and we all settled in to continue watching.

Further along in the movie, Sandra was trying on Betty White's vintage wedding dress, and the snoring started again. It was even louder this time, echoing across the theater and drowning out the voices on screen. The same girl who yelled before took charge.

"Yo! Wake up! We're trying to watch the movie! Shut up!"

A ripple went through the crowd, and Rob was clearly loving it. The snorer's girlfriend woke him again and the theater once again fell silent. The attention of three hundred people was trained on the screen. We were getting to the climactic scene. Ryan Reynolds was racing from Sitka, Alaska back to New York City. Ryan Reynolds was rushing into the office building to find Sandra Bullock and tell her that he really, truly—not for fear of getting fired, or to get her a green card—loved her. He ran into the elevator. He burst into the open-plan office. Magazine staffers lifted heads from desks and watched incredulously. Sandra Bullock, making her farewell walk with a cardboard box of her belongings after losing her job, turned around. Ryan and Sandra's eyes met.

The snoring started again.

The girl two rows ahead of us had had it. She stood halfway up in her seat, turned, and aimed an empty plastic Sprite bottle high in the air before chucking it directly at the snorer, like a right fielder pegging an overly ambitious asshole trying to turn a single into a double during an adult recreational softball game. She had impeccable aim, because the bottle hit the snorer's girlfriend, right next to him, and bounced off.

Someone let out a middle school style "Ooooooooooh." The snorer awoke and the noise stopped. We all turned back to the screen, settling in to enjoy the final scene now that business had been taken care of.

The silence didn't last long enough to catch Ryan's next line of dialogue. The girlfriend of the snoring guy suddenly appeared in front of us, leaping over the final seat to get to her attacker. There she was, two rows up, standing over the girl who had thrown the bottle. The girlfriend held up her movie-size-large plastic cup filled with ice and diluted Pepsi and dumped the entire thing over the girl's head.

Chaos ensued. The girl in front of us jumped up, reached into her jacket, and pulled out a knife, the blade flashing in the light of the movie screen. "I'll cut you!" she screamed, moving toward the snorer's girlfriend. "I'll cut you with my knife!" Knife Girl's boyfriend leapt up to hold her back. Snoring Guy had arrived and was holding his girlfriend back. The two girls were screaming and flailing, the hand with the knife flying all over.

Next to me, Rob the Tutee pulled out his phone and started filming.

As Rob held the phone high up, stretching his long arms to lean it toward the direction of the fight, I panicked. Knife girl was inches away from us. If she saw him filming, she might leap over the seat and start stabbing.

"Stop! Put it away!" I whispered, smacking his arm. Chrissy looked over and saw Rob with his phone. The scared look on her face turned into one of horror.

"No, this is great," the Tutee said aloud, face lit up with joy. I shrank further toward the floor. The rest of the theater was in uproar now, people trying to run out, everyone yelling. In front of us, Knife Girl wrenched herself free from the grip of her boyfriend to start chasing the other girl, who ran for the lobby, running right out of one Fioni by Payless leopard-print flat and leaving it behind in the aisle like a gangster Cinderella.

The boyfriends followed in a dead heat. The entire theater cleared out after them, while we stayed shellshocked in our seats. Onscreen, Ryan and Sandra were kissing, and I didn't know how it had happened. The credits started rolling.

The Tutee was still filming.

Chrissy and Kyle and I hustled out of there, past the chaos in the lobby, and straight out the front into the parking lot. Rob the Tutee lingered by the doors, probably hoping to catch any further action, and I yelled back at him that we were leaving.

As we drove home, I was certain of two things.

One, I needed to see the movie again to find out what happened with Ryan and Sandra.

Two, it might be time to cut ties with Rob the Tutee.

It had been an experiment, I told myself. Like when you give a wild animal an audition in a domestic situation. I didn't think it was going to work.

A year later, I thought I spotted him walking down South Street. I ducked into a coffee shop, trying to hide my face while peeking out the window to see if it was him. It was only a lookalike, though.

I did see *The Proposal* again—two more times. It's a very underrated film. Ryan and Sandra end up together. In case you were wondering.

Fresh Princess of Bel-Air

A BUNCH OF MY COMEDY friends were moving to Los Angeles. I decided to go too.

I worked seven days a week and saved three thousand in cash in an envelope. I kept the envelope in my desk drawer, and when I hit the target number, I wrote "You did it!" and doodled stars and palm trees around the words. My parents discussed renting out my bedroom. I packed up my silver Kia hatchback (the Saturn had choked to death by this point; I appreciate your concern) and drove cross-country.

The best part about driving across the country was feeling justified to eat whatever you wanted. I got pie at 3 pm in Flagstaff, Arizona. The waitress was a tiny woman with missing teeth. She said as she put the plate down, "Here's lookin' at you, kid." On my pie slice she had drawn a smiley face in whipped cream.

When I got to L.A., I went to a nanny agency to get a nine-to-five. I wore stockings and flats and a wrap dress to the office in West Hollywood, where a stack of books including *The Nanny Diaries* sat on a glass-topped desk. You could tell this agency chewed up young girls and spit them out.

The girl behind the desk was aggressively peppy. "You'd be a great candidate for the Musk family!" she said. "Elon Musk. They tend to go through nannies quickly, and they're looking for someone now! They're SO smart. They want someone who's smart!"

I spent a few days researching Elon Musk and found a video interview of him with his wife and the five kids. The whole family was wearing white shirts. Did I really want to work for someone who prioritized his nanny being "smart," as opposed to having the Marine-level psychological strength necessary to put up with his bullshit?

The agency emailed me with an interview opportunity. It wasn't for the Musks. I guess they did a background check on my AP Calculus performance (exam score: 1; drew comics in the answer spaces). Instead, it was a family who wanted a live-in nanny for a three-month period before they finished a temporary California stay. The details were my least desired circumstance: they didn't want the nanny to be alone with the child; both mother and grandmother would be around while I cared for a sixteen-month-old. But it was a short contract at twelve hundred dollars a week. I went Daffy Duck: pupils dilating into dollar signs.

I started planning all the things I could do with the money. Pay off credit card debt. Pay down my student loan. Get a real haircut. Go to the movies!

The multi-page document from the agency described rules for their nannies' appearance. Interview requirements: navy khakis, white polo shirt, white sneakers (dainty, please!). Hair: ponytail or otherwise tamed. Makeup: natural and conservative. All visible tattoos: covered. The instructions said to "look like the girl next door with a professional twist."

Ignoring the *Devil Wears Prada* (book version) quote to beware all enterprises that require new clothes (jacked from Thoreau, *I KNOW*), I slunk into a Banana Republic. I tried on navy khaki pants of a consistency heavier than I had worn in my entire life. The price tag was $86.

Do you know how much it hurt to carry $86 pants that I hated and didn't look good in to the register and hand over my debit card? I've never had a pet, but I felt like I was putting down a dog. The cashier put the pants into a sturdy bag with tissue paper and ribbon handles. Was this how all rich people shopped? They even got good bags? Did they even know what it was like to carry a plastic Walmart bag that rips before you get to the car? How many people were out there living this way?

Next I went to Target. I got a white polo shirt from the tween boys' section, clean white Keds, and a new conservative nude bra. Just in case.

At the Bel-Air mansion they buzzed my Kia through the security gate, and a guy in shorts with shoulder-length hair answered the door. I followed him through a maze of marble to a glossy wood-paneled office, where Nanny Mom sat behind a desk. A household staffer in uniform stood there with the toddler in her arms. I knew too well the awful game of performing for guests under the eyes of your boss. Nanny Mom was very nice, and I was called back for a second interview, this time with Nanny Mom's father.

The patriarch of the family sat behind the desk and grilled me. *Drink? Smoke? Drugs?* I held his gaze, pretending to myself that I had something to hide. *You want the truth?! YOU CAN'T HANDLE THE TRUTH!*

I was hired.

I went to Rite Aid and treated myself to a new bath pouf, tissues in the little packets, and some pink Suave body wash for the long haul of living in the palace. Then I browsed the shelf of paperbacks.

I was on a real chick-lit kick at the time. You know the type. Books with an illustration of a stiletto heel and champagne glass on the cover. Or the cozified down-home, older-woman version (muffin platter; yarn ball). Either way, I ate them up like candy. Time alone in motel rooms and sitting by bodies of water contemplating my future, and I was into the woman-hits-bottom-then-turns-life-around narrative. I bought two books to add to my current stock.

I moved into the palace. Phurpa, the long-haired house manager, gave me the lay of the land. As he talked, he called Nanny Mom "Madam" like we were in a BBC upstairs-downstairs colonial drama. The wheels on my suitcase echoed against the marble floor as I rolled it past black and white marble walls, gold statues, and a double staircase with gold handrails.

To reach the nanny chambers, I had to take multiple elevators. The first opened to the indoor pool room. (A bowling alley was another level up.) On the pool level, I walked along the edge of the pool deck and past squash courts on the far side to reach the second elevator. Sliding doors pushed open to my suite in the basement. It had a sitting area, kitchen, bedroom, and enormous bathroom. There were dozens of white drawers with shiny handles that opened smoothly. Phurpa told me with importance that when Prince Harry had visited, he'd stayed in my room.

"Madam" instructed me not to talk to the other household staff, particularly about what I was getting paid. There was no internet available in my nanny quarters downstairs, and my cell phone got no service anywhere on the grounds. I had one day off a week but was otherwise bound to the house. I was presented with a uniform: blue, white collar, white cuffs, white buttons.

The first couple days, I traveled with the baby, Madam, and Grandmother on outings to Rodeo Drive. I didn't love the Escalade, because it was so high up it was impossible to get into, but the white Rolls Royce was also a pain because the ceiling was so low it was tough to get the baby into her car seat without bumping her head. I couldn't find the seat belt for myself, or maybe there was none. I was going to die in a Rolls Royce while wearing a Mary Poppins uniform next to a toddler in Gucci. I did not want to go out like that. It wasn't on brand.

I pushed the stroller down Rodeo Drive in my uniform, following Madam and Grandmother as they went in and out of Tiffany & Co. and Cartier buying stuff for the baby. I was squinting, because I thought it wouldn't be appropriate to wear my five-dollar sunglasses. I had a Gucci diaper bag strapped across my chest and the baby's Gucci purse looped around my wrist.

On the second day, the baby spilled bubbles on her Juicy Couture pants. I looked in her closet to change them, but I didn't know what to do. Could I put Ralph Lauren pants with a Juicy top? Then she was pointing at Dolce & Gabbana shoes. Was it a faux pas to mix them? I was from northeast Philly; my knowledge of designer fashion stopped at the Forman Mills discount warehouse. (*"Stretch those bills!"*) I did have a Guess? sweatshirt once in high school, but that's not much to go on.

In my few moments alone with the kid, I propelled her up and down the expansive outdoor grounds in her little push car. I sang "Mister Sun" and imagined I was a British governess as we circled the stone fountains.

Phurpa cooked all the meals. On the third day while standing at attention spoon-feeding the baby, with Madam sitting and eating next to us, I let out the most delicate whisper of a fart. Madam's eyes flickered. After they finished, I ate my chicken and crispy rice in the other room.

I accompanied the family to a party at another mansion in the neighborhood. I wasn't sure how to act. Was the statue of the naked mermaid going to fall over if I accidentally knocked it with the diaper bag? Was I allowed to accept the appetizers offered me by the caterers, or was I supposed to downcast my eyes, indicating, *"Nay. I am but a servant"*? I didn't know what to do back at our palace, either. Was it okay that I disturb the tri-folded toilet paper or use one of the monogrammed hand towels in any of the twenty bathrooms in the house, or was I supposed to leave everything untouched and hold my pee until I could get to my own suite? Was I to wait until I was dismissed in the evening, or should I retire to my room when they took the baby to bed and I felt it was time to leave?

At the end of each day, I hunkered down in my nanny chambers. The humidity and scent of pool water was comforting as I walked through the dark and got onto the elevator. In the downstairs suite, I looked around at all the marble and drew out a calendar on paper so I could mark off days like a prisoner. *People do this; this will be like a meditative retreat. I can do it.* Within a day I metamorphosed into the girl in *Tangled*, filling her time with hobbies because there's no one to talk to. I colored in my sketchbook, cutting and pasting pictures of flowers from *Martha Stewart Weddings*. I didn't have a boyfriend per se, but I'd been talking to a ne'er-do-well ex, which had been enough to justify the purchase of the magazine. I settled in with my glue sticks.

In the mornings, the marble was cold on my feet, and I liked to duck-walk around the huge space in my underwear, just because I could, but at night, I spent a lot of time in the bathroom. The shower was green marble and vast, with a bench and ten shower heads. I sat under the shower heads, letting the water spray over me like a Rudyard Kipling hippo. There was also a Jacuzzi tub. Every night I filled it and sunk into the hot water with a loaf of bread and package of cheese slices on the side of the tub next to me, and read my chick lit. It was the only good part of the day. I finished *Sushi for Beginners* (hard-driving Dublin workaholic softens up when she finds unexpected love with new boss) and started *Shopaholic Ties the Knot* (flighty Brit plans lavish Manhattan wedding while her parents think they're hosting nuptials in backyard garden). I tried *The Inn at Rose Harbor* (widow takes over failing bed-and-breakfast; eligible bachelor from past hovers in wings) but it was so bad even I couldn't read it.

On the fourth day of pretending this was worth it, I went upstairs to the kitchen and knew I was done. I burst into tears. Phurpa came in and before I knew what was happening, I quit. I went down to my quarters to pack.

I emptied my things from the glossy drawers and filled my suitcase. I took off the uniform and put on my navy khakis. I hated this place, I hated Los Angeles, and I wanted to go home. There was a knock at the door. It was Phurpa.

I was still crying, and Phurpa came over and gave me a hug. Then the hug was lasting too long. He took both my hands and reached out with his thumb to wipe a tear from my eye.

Oh shit. Phurpa really did think we were in a BBC upstairs-downstairs colonial drama and that we were going to make a baby on Prince Harry's bed. I stepped away, got him out of there, closed the sliding doors and finished packing. I rolled my suitcase out of the palace and through the living room, past the new girl who had already arrived from the nanny agency, ready to take over the job and earn my twelve hundred dollars a week. I drove through the gates and away from the palace, headed straight for IHOP. I felt reborn.

I called my mom and said I was coming home. She said, "Of course you can come home! We have an exchange student from South Korea living in your old room, but we'll work it out."

For the journey back, I bought a new Fannie Flagg book. I don't know if you know her? She wrote *Fried Green Tomatoes*, which was made into a movie with Mary-Louise Parker and Kathy Bates. Fannie Flagg books were very comforting. Characters were retired southern women dealing with an empty nest or battling jaybirds in their front yard.

I liked to read at my solo dinners on the drive home, and I ate consistently at Cracker Barrel. I hit a Cracker Barrel in seven out of nine states. One night in Missouri, I was about to pull out my Fannie Flagg book at dinner, and I realized I was wearing my favorite red and white checkered flannel shirt. I knew that I couldn't be in Cracker Barrel, wear a red and white flannel, AND read a Fannie Flagg book at the same time. I could do two out of three, but not all of them. I ate my Chicken n' Dumplins and left the book in my bag.

I arrived back in Philly on a warm spring day. Because of the exchange student, I slept in my mom's office where I could almost touch all four walls if I stretched. My mom said, "Marth, I'm sorry about your broken dreams and all," (quick wave of hand: *that's taken care of*) "but when I heard you were coming home, I was thrilled!"

The exchange student and I coexisted for a few more weeks until she graduated high school and moved on. I finished the Fannie Flagg book. It wasn't her best, but it did the job.

A Good Party Guest Doesn't Get
Blood on the Carpet

IN 2006 I WENT TO a party on East 26th Street in New York City.

I lived in Washington Heights, running an afterschool program at the Y and renting a room for $600 a month. I had friends from college living in the East Twenties, and I took the A train down to the apartment of a guy they had known at school.

I went to college at the University of Pennsylvania, where you couldn't throw a pencil without hitting someone's monogram. The spread included Chaz, who at eighteen sat on a wall outside the dorm daily eating a banana and reading *The Wall Street Journal*; a fraternity known as The Castle because it was; and, regrettably, Ivanka Trump. Being a scholarship kid from Philly, it was jarring for me to see guys wearing pink pants without fear of getting beat up. I found friends who I clicked with. But no matter how you tried to avoid it, if you were hanging in Penn circles you were always going to come across somebody you wouldn't normally choose to be around.

The end result was that during my first year in New York I sometimes wound up at parties where a guy in white linen pants would say, "I work hard, but I play hard, too."

The most significant birdcall was when someone introduced themselves as an "i-banker." This was short for "investment banker," I learned, and tipped you off that you were in the presence of a New York Finance Bro, and you should walk away now and go get a pepperoni slice on the corner. They're open twenty-four hours; it's great.

Our party host Dylan was, in fact, an i-banker for one of Wall Street's biggest financial institutions. It was the only bank that would go on to have someone face jail time for their role in the subprime mortgage crisis that caused the Great Recession; the ruling judge called it "a small piece of an overall evil climate within the bank and with many other banks." Along with selling toxic mortgage-backed securities, this company pleaded guilty in helping wealthy customers evade taxes, and for numerous violations of research analyst conflict of interest rules.

I'm not saying the entry-level recruits we came across were important enough to be involved in anything greasy. But they were proud to be devoted to a culture whose purpose was to help the rich get richer, legality and morality be damned. Money was their religion, their language, and their status symbol. I can name a handful of guys I knew who worked in finance who were tolerably decent. I probably met a hundred who weren't.

Years later, when I saw *The Wolf of Wall Street* and watched Leonardo DiCaprio's character tossing thousands of dollars off his boat just because he could, I remembered meeting a Penn grad banker who pulled fistfuls of bills out of his wallet in a diner at midnight, throwing them in the air like confetti and stumbling out. In 2006, I didn't know anything about financial corruption, but on pure observation I could conclude that most of these people were assholes.

But. I was twenty-three and had just moved to New York. If I was invited to a party, I went.

So I walked with my friend Beck to Dylan's apartment. I'd met Dylan a couple times in college, and had never seen him without a baseball cap. It was bizarre greeting a hatless Dylan in his grownup apartment that he shared with a coworker. They had cleared the living room for the party, pushing black leather furniture to the side to display an open field of parquet wood floor. Next to the giant TV, an IKEA floor lamp was in the corner with the cord hanging out for anyone to trip over. Some bottles of booze and red Solo cups were in the kitchen. There were no snacks.

We said hi to another college friend, Eric, and he told us that Joey Weinberg, who always got drunk enough to provide a night of entertainment, was on the way. There was a sprinkling of Finance Bros from Dylan's workplace, along with some New York Marketing Girls gripping cocktails and Zara clutch bags in tight bootcut jeans, bright silk cowl neck tanks, and sparkly eyeshadow.

I ended up in a small circle that included one of Dylan's coworkers who had clearly already had a lot to drink.

People were cracking jokes about each other's ages. I said something about how the drunk guy clearly wasn't that old—some type of banter, a compliment. Drunk Guy misunderstood. He thrust his chin toward me and sneered.

"You're not very good looking," he said. "You're out of shape."

I stared. Maybe my mouth fell open, I don't know. "Not good looking," he repeated. "Out of shape."

Fact check: I was not out of shape (to be fair, my standards may have differed slightly from the Marketing Girls), and I am *very* good looking. Regardless. Polite party conversation shouldn't stray further from talking about your job or discovering you have Mike Keutmann from Poughkeepsie in common. Hadn't he read *Bridget Jones's Diary*, which details clear instructions on how to mingle?

I was so stunned that I took a couple steps back and walked away. I found Beck and my brain started to process what had just happened. Did this nerd wearing a button-down on a Saturday night really just say that to me?

—Yes. He did. I digested the reality. I thought for a second, made my decision, walked over to where the guy was standing with his friends, and punched him in the side of the head.

He stumbled backwards, falling halfway down at the impact, his eyes frozen wide like a moose stunned in the Alaskan wild. I purposely hadn't gone for the nose. I knew a nose punch hurts like nothing else and could result in a lot of blood. Blood is messy, and I was a guest. But as soon as I connected, I realized I hadn't contemplated the result of a punch delivered incorrectly against a skull. I knew immediately that my hand was broken.

The state of my hand didn't matter right now, though. I threw my other arm up and out in the universal "come at me bro" gesture that he likely thought was a stock exchange floor hand signal.

I turned around and met the eyes of a room full of Finance Bros and Marketing Girls shocked into silence. All the air went out of the room in the equivalent of a record scratch. I walked casually back to my friends, holding my injured hand at waist level to pretend I wasn't in pain. It was starting to creep over me, like I'd been snake-bit, and I could feel my eyes getting wild and darting around as I tried to make my body act completely relaxed.

"Oh my God Martha!" Beck said, mouth hanging open.

"Do you want to go …" I started quietly, then looked around. Strangers were staring. I leaned toward Beck's ear and murmured, "to the emergency room? Like, not yet. In a bit."

Beck rummaged a bag of peas from the freezer, and I laid it on my hand, trying to keep it subtle. After Eric went over and demanded an apology, Drunk Guy stumbled toward us. "Sorry," he sneered in the same tone as you would say "Asshole," wobbling to his left like a Russian doll. "Whatever," I snapped, turning away, and he went back to his side of the room, plummeting midway and barely catching himself on the leather couch.

Somehow, the party continued, and more guests arrived. I made sure not to leave until I'd stood around in a laid-back manner for long enough to prove that Drunk Guy hadn't won. As Beck and I were about to head out the door, Joey Weinberg staggered in, fell into the radiator, hit his head and bled all over the floor. After I had been so careful, too.

I spent the night on Beck's couch, struggled to dress myself in the morning, and walked over to the NYU hospital emergency room where I had to tell one hospital staffer after another how I got my injury.

The first doctor, a man in his sixties, gave me a disgusted look. He said, "Why would you do a thing like that?"

The second doctor was a tall and gawky redhead in his residency. He told me that I had broken the fifth metacarpal on my left hand. It was known as a boxer's fracture. He said I'd need a cast for six weeks, and thoroughly explained the process as he wrapped the plaster cast and described the dissolution and hardening method of the chemicals. When he finished, he dismissed me with a smile and said, "Be careful out there."

I met Beck down the street for a dinner of sweet potato fries. "Do you think I could sue that guy for what he said to me?" I mused. "Um, it's definitely more like he could sue you," Beck said.

I took the subway to my apartment on 200th Street and faced life with a cast on my dominant hand. I'd never broken a bone before. I fixed a plastic bag to the cast with a rubber band to shower and found it impossible to tie my hair back. At work, I told my boss I had injured my hand in an accidental taxi door slam, but this would certainly not hold me back from doing my job.

I typed with one finger on my left hand. I tried using my right hand to write; it took forever and was a kindergarten scrawl, but it was my only option. I got through my first day back at work.

That night at home, I got a call on my T-Mobile flip phone from a number I didn't recognize. A trembling voice on the other end said, "Martha? This is Jim. Um, the guy who said some pretty terrible things to you the other night?"

Oh ho ho.

I straightened up, holding the phone awkwardly with my right hand. I started pacing my room. "Yeah?"

"I got your number from Dylan," he started nervously. "My friends told me what I said to you, and I don't remember any of it, and I am so sorry. And I heard you broke your hand, and I'm so sorry that that happened, and I've been doing a lot of soul searching the past few days …"

Excuse me?

"… and I realized if I got so drunk that I could do something like that, and not remember it, that I must have a problem, and I'm going to do something about it. And you probably never want to see me again, but maybe you could take down my number and we could meet up and you could see that I'm not such a bad guy."

"Well," I said, "I would take down your number, but I have a cast on my hand so I can't write right now."

"I'm so sorry about that," he said. I let it sit.

Finally I said, "Why don't you text me your number and we'll see."

"Okay, I will. Thank you."

A text popped up immediately after I snapped the phone shut. It was Jim, thanking me for talking and repeating his offer to meet up. I wrote back. *It took balls to call, sure we could meet up sometime.* There. I'd reassured him that I wasn't interested in taking the battle any further. No way were we going to ever meet up. That was that.

A few days later, he texted again. *I'm free on Sunday. Do you want to meet at Starbucks?*

What was this? Was it revenge? Would he have legions of investment bankers ready to attack with briefcases? Or was this going to be the best how-we-met story ever, to be featured in *The New York Times* Vows section? Was he so tortured by the idea of someone knowing he was an asshole that he felt the need to clear his name across all five boroughs?

I called Beck for backup. She agreed to go with me, and on Sunday, we met Jim in the Starbucks on 29th street. He was there already, with a table for three. Beck and I got coffee and joined him.

My cast was poking out visibly from my jacket sleeve, and I immediately referenced it with a joke. Jim looked so guilty, and so nervous, that I felt bad for him. Beck was the perfect partner when it came to talking to people, so the two of us moved things along with cheerful getting-to-know-you conversation, and Jim started to relax. We found out that Jim was from Canada, that he had a girlfriend, and that he preferred his cappuccino bone dry. I told him about my job at the afterschool program. We chatted for about an hour. When it was time to wrap up, I looked him in the eye and said, "I'm sorry I hit you." He said, "I'm sorry I said those things."

We left. Back in the apartment, Beck and I found Jim on Facebook and friended him.

After my cast came off, my left hand was forever missing its baby knuckle, but otherwise it recovered beautifully, with just a twinge here and there when rain was in the forecast. When my birthday rolled around that year, I planned to host a party at a bar, and sent out a Facebook invite. Just to make him uncomfortable, I included Jim on the invitation.

He wrote back:

> *Thank you very much for inviting me to your birthday. Unfortunately I am tied up on Saturday and won't be able to attend.*
>
> *How's everything going? Are you still working for the Y? Things are going well on my end. Work is fine, but a bit slow. Trying to make the most out of the summer, even though I can't stand to go outside with the humidity.*
>
> *Stay in touch,*
> *Jim*

I lived in New York for three more years, and every year I invited Jim to my birthday. Just so he would never forget what had happened.

By the way, Beck made a painting that reinterpreted Joey Weinberg's bloody fall into the radiator. She titled it "The Accident."

Love Thy Neighbor

During the winters when I was a kid, my mother kept a broom just inside the front door. The neighbors' cat, Muffin, liked to wait on the porch on cold mornings and spring herself inside the house when Mom opened the door to get the newspaper. Twice Muffin made it up two flights to the attic before my mother chased her out. Mom was a soft-spoken Catholic school children's librarian, but she could turn vicious when called for.

Every morning, Mom would pick up the broom, open the screen door an inch and push the straw bristles through, saying "Shoo! Shoo!" If the paper was close to the house, Mom would keep eyes on Muffin and jab the broom toward her with one hand while the other swiped blindly at the ground. Once she got a grip, she eased the paper in behind the broom, then did a slow-motion withdrawal of bristles to close the door.

If the *Inquirer* deliverer had done a half-hearted throw, Mom had to get her whole body onto the porch broom-first, shut the door, walk over to get the paper from the front yard and then re-enter the house. Muffin knew her own odds for success were doubled. My mother got more aggressive. She celebrated loudly every time she made it into the house catless.

In warmer temperatures, Muffin preferred the outdoors. She was gray and beefy, all fluff, and she owned the block, hiding under front-lawn bushes and staring down any human who approached her sunning zone on the sidewalk. She crossed deliberately in front of cars in a slow-hipped walk, giving off the jaywalker power eye: *I got the right of way. Try me.*

Muffin's owners lived on the other side of our twin house. They had four kids who, like Muffin, had the run of the neighborhood. Anthony, the youngest, was the smallest on our block, but cursed out teenagers and held court on his fun-sized bike. There was a tree in their backyard, and I watched one summer day as Anthony sat up there with a handsaw, hacking at the branch he was sitting on.

I had goals of my own. At nine years old, I kept eyes and ears to the ground as publisher and beat reporter of a hard-hitting local newspaper (circulation: 1). I spent most of my time on the headlines (*Chromie Fever*; *What's with Movies?*) and completed one investigative report detailing recent street brawls. We all knew everything that was going on in the neighborhood, because we had nothing else to do. Kids gathered to spy, climb chain-link fences between yards, sneak attack with Super Soakers, hustle money, ride bikes, and fistfight. I feel for today's children who only participate in organized activities. There's no dance camp that can compete with the thrill of throwing pennies on the train tracks and waiting for them to get flattened. If I wanted to pedal my sweet self to a vacant lot and sit on the gravel pretending to be Roald Dahl's Matilda moving things with her eyeballs, there was no virtual breadcrumb trail or adult watching from a lawn chair to kill the vibe. Our mothers had no idea where we were, and we were free, baby, free! Riding bikes without helmets, chomping candy cigarettes, laughing our way into the sunset.

Muffin parked herself in the outfield during street Wiffle ball games, and as she got older, she spent a lot of time in our driveway, leaving gifts of dead mice on the front porch. She started sleeping under cars on hot days, and Amanda Byrne's mom accidentally ran over her. It was a shame, but I think she was ready to go. The neighbors got another pet, a Rottweiler named Lucky. Visitors came to their house often, and Lucky barked around the clock.

We knew not to get too chummy with Anthony's dad. One day after an argument, he walked out front and shot all the windows out of his wife's parked car. Thinking about it now, I'm sure he was the one who ended up fixing the windows, because he worked at an auto body shop. *Joke's on you.*

Lucky kept his bark up as the kids on the block grew, put away the Super Soakers and splintered off. When I was in high school, the neighbors got backyard chickens. I looked out our kitchen window onto the coop every night as I washed dinner dishes. I had always had a childhood fantasy of living on a farm. It wasn't an exact match.

I moved across the city for college. When I came home for Easter during my sophomore year, there was a floral wreath on the neighbors' door spelling out Lucky's name. My mom filled me in with a child's animation: she loved being the first to tell. Police had raided the house the week prior, kicked in the door, and shot the dog. They didn't find the drugs they were looking for, though. Poor Lucky. It was quiet next door except for the chickens squawking out back. We ate our ham and pineapple.

A couple weeks later, I stopped by again for dinner. The neighbors' house was boarded up, and the chickens had been taken away. "Marth, wait'll you hear," Mom said, excited. The feds had come back and this time they found everything. The meth lab was shut down.

My mother put her palm in the air as if eager to give an answer in class. "I knew it," she said proudly, squaring her shoulders under her t-shirt that read, in Google-style font, *Librarian: The Original Search Engine.* "I smelled something. Didn't I say it, I smelled something? I heard him hammering. He was hiding stuff in the walls."

It was unnerving to realize I'd underestimated my mother. I thought I had better street smarts than her. Had she always known more than I thought she did? Worse, she'd scooped me. The biggest news in the neighborhood had been right under my nose and I'd missed it.

A few weeks ago, she had a new one. "Marth, look," she said, pulling out a newspaper article she'd saved. "Verree Pharmacy up the street, the guy got sentenced for pushing more Oxy than anywhere else in the country. Remember, you guys used to buy candy there?" She still loved that we were close to any action.

Like she always does, she'd written across the top of the clipping in pen: *The Philadelphia Inquirer, October 4, 2022.* Just in case I got pulled over and the cop asked me to cite my sources.

You Too Can Work in Catering: A Guide

You TOO CAN WORK IN catering and serve dinner at big weddings in an elegant event space. Follow the steps below.

THE SETUP

Show up to the ballroom you are helping set up for tonight's wedding. Find someone who knows what they're doing. Play Whisper Down the Lane with the rest of the team about which tables are going where. Eavesdrop on a groomsman's conversation with the DJ. He'll talk about how he wishes he were a DJ. The DJ will ask what he does, and he'll say, "Private equity finance. Boring, I know." Two of your managers who hate each other will give conflicting directions on the table linens. Never, ever choose a side. Find something else to do. Go fold napkins. They are in a trifold tonight. Not a swan fold. Know the difference. Someone who's better at folding napkins will tell you that your folds are getting a little puffy. Escape to the back to put ice in glasses.

Spend some time with the kitchen guys for a standard food industry 50/50 blend of sexual harassment and good clean fun.

THE FOOD MEETING

Before the guests arrive, assemble with the servers to go over the menu. Do not ask your shift leader to borrow a pen; she will not be happy. Chef Kenneth will lead the food meeting. He's the opposite of Gordon Ramsay. Gordon Ramsay explodes at his staff and says that a piece of cooked fish looks like Gandhi's flip flop. Kenneth answers all questions with a warm smile and delivers a podcast's worth of inspiration on how corn fungus is harvested and prepared. By the time he's done, you've added a Bon Appétit subscription to your Christmas list.

SERVING THE APPETIZERS

Study the following types of guests you will encounter while serving appetizers. You'll learn how to deal with each of them.

The Interviewer: This guest wants to know everything about what's on your platter. They'll call you over and start by commenting on the aesthetics. "How cute! The grilled cheese bite is right on top of the shot glass of tomato soup! That's adorable!" They have some more questions. What kind of cheese is it? Is that challah bread? Sourdough? Does the bread have butter on it? Is there cream in the soup? Is it spicy? Is it very hot? The Interviewer has studied the five Ws of journalism and will come up with a few more questions. After they find out the cooking process and your opinion of how it tastes (walk the line here), they're satisfied. That's when they will say "No, thanks," and wave their hand with a flat smile to dismiss you.

The Hungry Bear: This guy is on your side. There's one in every crowd, and your job is to locate him and make him your friend. He's thrilled to see you coming. He'll grab several pork belly skewers and push everyone in his circle to take some. "You guys gotta try these!" The key is to treat him like a VIP.

When you finally serve the shrimp cocktail after you've done multiple rounds with quiches, give him first dibs. Joke about how he's helping you do your job. A win for everybody.

The Aristocrat: This guest is absolutely appalled that you would invite them to eat bruschetta on a Melba toast round, and they are not afraid to let you know. Sometimes they'll raise a hand in a reverse karate chop and snap, "NO." Other times it will just be a tight head shake, or—a personal favorite—the scornful laugh. Since you don't know where an Aristocrat will pop up, it's best to appear non-threatening at all times. Make no sudden movements and offer all invitations in a muted, placating tone: "Date with bacon?" The key is to avoid any trace of aggression, as you don't want the Aristocrat to think you are challenging them. When you do happen upon one, you'll know. They are not just saying no. They are *angry*. Leave them alone! Get the platter out of their face! Don't you know who they are? If they wanted scallops, they would order their own iced barrel! They're not trying to be part of this Oliver Twist gruel line! Your job is to maintain a gentle smile and nod, delicately withdraw the tray, and float away in a seamless *Swan Lake* transition.

The Normal Guy: This guy doesn't have time for food world flim-flam. You'll murmur "Vichyssoise?" and he'll bark, "WHAT? WHAT'S THAT?" There are two choose-your-own-adventure options. You can give up the game and say in your regular voice, "It's potato soup." Or you can repeat, in an exaggerated tone, "*VISHY-SWA*? It's a mingling of leek and onion pureed with Yukon gold potatoes, in a cream base blended with chicken stock. And it has a garnish of chopped fresh chives." Either way, Normal Guy will shrug and decide to give it a try. He'll cram a meaty hand in between the rows of delicately balanced glass vials, trying to grip one with his thick Jimmy Deans. Plant your feet to hold the platter steady. You know you're both wishing these were hot dogs on cardboard trays, but please, don't say so aloud.

The Sinner: This guest puts more thought into accepting an appetizer than she would to getting a tattoo. It is extremely important to her to let you know that she thinks she SHOULD NOT accept the invitation to eat said appetizer. There's an entire therapy session in the transaction. She may audibly shout, "Ugh! Oh my God!" when you offer your platter. Remain neutral. This is part of the process. There will be a physical transformation: hunching over, squinting, tightening the mouth into "I want to do this, but SHOULD I?" She'll look to the rest of the group for support. After conferencing, the Sinner purses her lips and gives a heavy sigh. "I guess I'll have one," she'll say shamefully. Then she will reach delicately toward the platter and pluck a mushroom tart with two fingers as if picking up an eyeball with tweezers. The rest of the group stays stock still, leaving her out on a limb with a mouth full of buttery crust. An interaction with the Sinner always leaves you feeling guilty. Try not to watch as she chews with knitted brows. Let her bear the burden alone.

The Ringleader: The strategy here is boldness. Approach a group and insert your tray at a pre-identified weakness in the circle, like breaking a Red Rover line. Announce yourself: "Kobe beef?" Let the words hang. Don't rush off; the circle will take some time to carry out their group dynamic. There will be a general bodily freeze. Some will stare at your platter, not daring to make a move. Others will check in with each other with quick and fearful eye movements. Finally, the Ringleader says, "I'll go for it," and reaches out. Four additional hands will fly toward the food in one quick movement to display enthusiasm for the leader's decision. The Ringleader vocally enjoys their bite of meat, and the others chime in on how delicious it is. The Ringleader is on the same Venn diagram as the Hungry Bear, but the Ringleader is more fully aware of his power.

The Pity Party: This guest is just so sorry that they can't help you out. They see you lurking and say, "What do we have here?" to humor you. They listen to your hopeful description and say, "No thanks," but give the consolation prize, "It looks good though."

CHECK YOUR TABLES

Check orders before dinner to make sure everyone is seated in the right spot. Hover behind couples having intimate conversations to see if they have put out their meal cards with the graphic of a sad cow or perky chicken. The count will always be off. A girl who is used to having exceptions made for her, likely a cousin to the bride, will lean close to you. "Uncle Sherman stayed. Uncle Sherman wasn't gonna stay. Uncle Sherman messed up the count." Interview girl to figure out where the hell Uncle Sherman is supposed to be. Track down Uncle Sherman. Cause family argument. Do mental math, write down order totals and go back to the kitchen.

BROKEN GLASS

After dinner, guests are going to start getting wild. When someone drops a glass and it breaks, create a safe zone around the mess and call in a friend for backup. While they get a broom, stand over the glass in the middle of the room as drunk people dance around you. Do not tell the couple nearest you to leave room for the Holy Spirit. Get down on hands and knees to gather the biggest pieces. A guy will come over and start Riverdancing on top of the broken glass while people clap around him. Feel free to get a good grip on his calf muscle and shove him as hard as you can.

EATING

Operate as a team with your fellow servers. Give others the heads up if a tray of untouched dinner rolls is up for grabs. At the same time, look out for yourself and go for it when you have the chance. If a coworker you've never been introduced to holds out a skewer of unknown meat and your hands are full of dirty plates, open your mouth and let them poke it in. Think about how you're going to approach the evening. Are you willing to eat something off a plate that was served but hasn't been touched? Remember these cuts of beef are worth sixty bucks apiece. Your apron pocket is deep and can hold lots of macarons for later. There's no right way or wrong way, but for efficiency's sake, do some goal setting ahead of time.

CLEARING THE ROOM

Over the course of the event, you will transform from Gracious Server to Surly Waitress. This is natural. Let it ride. While it's still early in the evening, do your best to clear dirty glasses in a subtle manner, taking care not to disturb anyone's elbow space. By the end of the night, your hand will become an arcade game claw descending in the middle of someone's conversation to snatch a glass. Do not care. Keep going.

When the DJ plays "Sweet Caroline," you're in the end zone. After the bar closes, watch the groom try to steal bottles from behind the bar. When the bartender stops him, he will fight his way into the kitchen. "I want a couple bourbon neats. This is MY wedding. This is MY wedding. You're ruining everything." Don't get distracted. The lights are on now. As soon as someone's bottom leaves a chair to search for an abandoned high heel, whisk the chair out from under them and shove it toward the wall to start stacking.

Approach a guy clutching a martini glass and talking to a woman. Ask him, "Can I take your glass?" Do not break eye contact as he looks right at you and says ever so coolly, "Actually, I'm not finished with it yet." Accept that it has become a power play. The wedding is over, the room is being packed up, but the gentleman is staking a claim to his right to continue drinking his martini. Stare hard at his girlfriend. Stare hard at him. Walk away and circle the room one more time, practicing the angry line of dialogue you will deliver. Prepare for a fight. Finish your circling and stride back to the gentleman's table. The martini glass will be sitting there empty. He'll be walking away.

The night's over, so wrap some rolls in a napkin and go to the bar. You lost the battle. You won the war. Don't forget to clock out.

Lost by the Gentlemen's Club

I HAD THIS PARKING SPOT on South Broad between the Popeye's and the RiteAid. It was on a small stretch of curb in between the two store driveways, and the signage wasn't exactly clear. If you really pushed me, I'd say the signs indicated no parking. The first time I took a chance, I didn't get a ticket. No ticket the second time either. I parked in that spot a few times a week without a problem.

This went on for a couple years. Other people arrived late to meetings or rehearsals, breathing heavily, "I couldn't find parking." I shrugged and said, "I have this secret spot."

Nobody cared to get advice from me, a native Philadelphian, but I gave it out freely anyway, so no one would forget that I was here first. Get Steve's Prince of Steaks instead of Pat's or Geno's. For pizza you want to get Allegro's on 40th. The best soft pretzels are only sold out of shopping carts on the street. When it comes to parking, you have to figure out where the loopholes are.

One day I had some business in Center City. I drove to Broad, parked in my spot, went off, and came back. My car was gone.

I felt as if a boyfriend of ten years had forgotten my birthday. I wanted to call up the Philadelphia Parking Authority and say, "Hey, it's me. What happened?" I thought we had a deal.

Okay. I had to get my Kia back. I knew the location of the PPA tow lot, so I looked up the cross streets and got the bus down to Oregon Ave. I stood in a long line of other unfortunate people waiting to retrieve their cars. I stepped up to the window and they looked up my information.

My car wasn't there. It had been taken to a tow place across the city at 39th and Girard.

I decided that I knew where I was going, and I would make my way there without looking up a specific bus route. I knew where 39th and Girard was. I'd just get a bus going west, and when I got into the thirties I would get off and catch a bus going north. It wasn't that complicated.

I went to the bus stop at the corner and got on the first SEPTA bus that came along. It was empty, and I got a window seat in the solid middle of the bus. At the next couple stops a good number of people got on, and someone took the seat next to me. I had to move my backpack. I had an enormous backpack, since I'd expected to only be on foot for a few blocks that day. It was as stuffed as a bag carried by a short-in-stature high schooler taking five Advanced Placement courses and when jostled while traveling from the third floor to the second tumbles all the way down the staircase due to the sheer weight on their back. (Net force is equal to mass times acceleration. Newton's Second Law.)

I decided to shove my big backpack onto the floor between my seat and the seat in front. I positioned my feet on top of it. The puffy jacket and extended elbows of the person next to me had me pinned to the window.

There are rules on a SEPTA bus. You don't make bodily contact with anyone. If it's unavoidable, do not make eye contact at the same time. Avert your eyes, stare out the window, and pretend you are piloting a plane solo through a cumulonimbus cloud.

I kept my head turned, waiting for us to get to a spot westward enough for me to get off. The bus moved down Oregon and passengers continued to crowd on at every stop. It was full now. People stood in the aisle packed in like a New York subway. All of a sudden, the bus took a turn south and gained speed. I no longer recognized where we were. Rows of houses disappeared, and a gray industrial stretch appeared before us. We weren't making stops anymore. The driver barreled along, making time like we were in *Speed* (Sandra Bullock, 1994).

One brain cell on duty in command central pressed a neon button and cleared her throat. "*Attention! You don't know where this is going and you're getting lost. You need to get off the bus.*"

Another brain cell popped up from a ball pit, holding a Mountain Dew Big Gulp. "*Let's just see where it goes! Why not? Stay on the bus! You'll magically get to your destination!*"

For ten minutes the brain cells argued. "*She needs to get off! You're getting hoagie juice on my blazer!*" "*You're boring! Everything will work out! Did you know your hand is bigger than your face?*"

I was frozen in my seat. I didn't recognize anything, but I kept waiting to see if I would recognize something soon. Should I go in my bag for my phone to figure it out? This was not an easy proposition. Unearthing the phone from the deep pocket in my bag would be a process. I would have to disturb the equilibrium with my neighbor. Moving my body would be acknowledging that our bodies were in fact touching, and continuing to shuffle around as I went into my bag would stretch that acknowledgement out for an uncomfortable length of time. I'd have to do a real dive to unzip the bag, and my elbows would poke into my seatmate. Plus, the bag was so full that it would take some unpacking to get to the phone. On top was my jacket, stuffed in, and it would expand to eight times its size once removed from the bag. Under the jacket was a book, *Nice Girls Don't Get the Corner Office*. I didn't want to take that out and hold it in full view of other passengers. They'd think I was a nerd.

There were also binders Sharpied with exclamation points, a laptop case, notebooks, a Tupperware with the shell of a hard-boiled egg, and a water bottle. I couldn't do it. I stared out the window and accepted the journey I was on. The second brain cell, satisfied, dove back into the ball pit.

We traveled another ten minutes before I knew we were truly approaching the end of the world. It was *Erin Brockovich* territory (Julia Roberts, 2000). Blank gray towers belching smoke, intermittent trash dumps, empty lots parked with derelict trucks. The place was a wasteland. I couldn't believe we were in a part of the city I didn't recognize. Why had they kept this from me? Were we even in Philly anymore? Had the bus time traveled? I made a move. I pulled the bell to get off.

Getting off the bus with a full backpack is a misery beyond making physical contact with your seatmate. I said, "Excuse me," to my neighbor, reached down to extract the bag from between the seats, and hauled it up. I couldn't avoid hitting three people with it as I strapped it to my body. Then I took two minutes to make my way to the front, bumping everyone with the bag as I went. The bus was so full, and the process took so long, that the entire bus of people were watching by the time I stepped off the bus and saw the building in front of me, the only building for miles, which they must have assumed was the reason I got off with my enormous bag. I looked up at the sign. It was a strip club.

The bus zoomed off. I stood on the corner in front of the strip club and looked around. Highway, desolation, a pile of junk cars across the street. I had the elbow space now to go into my bag and get my phone out to figure out where the hell I was. I opened the web browser. It was 2015. Rideshare apps had been available for a couple years, but I didn't have any on my phone. I didn't believe in Uber at the time.

I figured I would google a taxi company and get a cab. I looked up a place and called. On the second ring, my phone died.

Okay. I looked up and down the road. Would I hitchhike? Was I someone who could successfully complete a hitchhike? I could try. What do you do, I wondered. Do you just kind of flop your arm out and rotate your wrist a little? Do you show a little ankle like she did in *It Happened One Night*? (Claudette Colbert, 1934).

I approached the edge of the road and extended my hand in a half-hearted wave. *Pardon me. Seem to have lost my way.* The cars were all going seventy because no one else wanted to be on this stretch of road either. The sky, ground, air, metalwork, trash, fencing was gray. It was the most depressing place I'd ever been.

Okay. I would walk.

Twelve summers I'd worked at outdoor camps leading kids through the woods. I tried to remember what we'd taught them. Didn't we say moss grew on the north side of trees? That's how you could tell which way you were going? There were no trees here, though. I'd completely bullshitted those children. I had no survival skills. I couldn't orient myself out of an unknown location. I knew the sun set in the west, but right now it was cloudy.

I took a guess which way was north. I started walking.

On both sides of the street were a stretch of junkyards straight out of Stephen King. Lot after lot of rusty vehicle carcasses. Scrap heaps, tire stacks, barbed wire fences protecting it all. No one had been here since the seventies. Was this the Apocalypse? I looked through every fence, expecting a tough broad in a canvas jumpsuit to hear me snooping around and come out to investigate, cigarette in mouth, one hand holding a bottle of Wild Turkey and the other a half-eaten sandwich (Stroehmann white bread, Dietz and Watson baloney, Hellman's). There was no one.

I walked and walked and walked. This would be the perfect murder. No one would find my body parts. They'd go in that stack of tires over there. It was getting dark. My phone was dead. Nobody knew where I was.

The most frustrating part was that I knew exactly the conversations my family and friends would have if I died. *"Of course her car was towed, she didn't ask for directions, and her phone wasn't charged. Are we sad? Yeah. Yeah. We are. We are. Are we surprised? No. No. No, no."*

Everyone would be so focused on the circumstances of the death that I'd be cheated out of them remembering my Halloween costume collection and my signature vodka Jell-O cake. It wasn't fair.

I walked on. Woods popped up to my left. I saw a human, walking his dog, but my brain was fixated now, and I ignored him. *Just gotta walk north.* I was in a neighborhood again, with rows of houses, and it threw me off. Was I still going in the right direction? Streetlights buzzed to life above me and lights switched on from living room windows. I wandered like a seven-year-old refusing to come home for dinner. By the time I tumbled onto Baltimore Avenue, blinking and disoriented, I'd been lost for three hours.

A cab came by, and I grabbed it. The driver took me to the tow place at 39th and Girard. I walked in, relieved, and half fell across the counter. The guy shook his head. Cash only.

Okay. I went to the corner store across the street, got two hundred and fifty bucks out of the ATM, and returned to the window. He gave me a handwritten receipt, pointed, and hit the button to roll up the metal grate. There it was. I got in my car and sat in it.

How embarrassing. I was supposed to be a local. I couldn't tell anybody about this ever.

I drove to Allegro's Pizza on 40th, got two slices of plain, and ate them in the car. After that, I stopped parking in my secret spot. Do I have a new one? Come on. You think I would tell you where it was if I did?

I Know, But Mary Poppins
Actually Flew

I ONCE WORKED ON NEW York City's Upper East Side as a nanny for a toddler who knew how to do all kinds of things I didn't. Carter could hail a cab on Madison Avenue and wear a monogram. He could tip a dollar to a doorman named Rusty and pull off a Russian fur cap with confidence. I was twenty-four and Carter's mom, Lisa, wanted me to do a lot of things I found questionable.

Carter was sixteen months old. Lisa instructed me to take him to lunch daily at restaurants with names like Sant Ambroeus. She had me take him in cabs without car seats to Diller-Quayle Music School ("collaborative music making with peers"; Carter's uniform: Burberry pants) and Free to Be Under Three class ("usually a wait of no more than six months to be offered a spot"; Converse sneakers for a casual look). Lisa wanted me to ask the teacher of Carter's gymnastics class if they could start a separate "advanced" class for his age group. She asked me to call the adult daughter of her Polish cleaner, Barbara, and have her translate directions for a more thorough wash of Carter's sippy cups. I did not like any of these ideas. But I was earning twenty dollars an hour, so I did as Lisa wished. Plus, she gave me a credit card for unlimited spending on my own meals during the day. I brought Tupperwares and ate free leftovers every night in my un-air-conditioned 152nd Street apartment.

Many times, Carter would stay at home with Lisa while she dispatched me on some type of errand. Once I was sent across town to put a deposit down on a grand piano. She gave me an envelope with ten thousand dollars cash inside it and put me in the back of a limousine.

I did not feel calm. I was afraid to touch the envelope but also afraid to not be always touching the envelope. What if this money spontaneously combusted? What if the driver forcibly took the money from me; what was stopping him? What if I got out of the car and a gust of wind sent the bills flying like a ticker tape parade? What if I got the money into the piano guy's hand, but he said I never paid him? It was my word against his.

The payment went fine. Three days later, the piano was delivered by pulleys through the fourteenth-floor window.

Lisa's next project was Carter's Halloween party. She was renting out a puppet theater in Central Park. I went to the theater to take measurements of the windows so the spider webbing would be cut to the inch. I procured a Superman costume for Carter and brought the costume to the tailor to get it custom fit. The caterer prepped grilled cheese sandwiches in the shape of ghosts. Lisa ordered five hundred purple balloons to fill the ceiling.

The day of the party, I went in a limo to fetch the singer they hired, Bobby Valentine—not his real name—and deliver him to the theater. Lisa was wearing a witch's hat. She handed me another one and told me to put it on. I did. For most of the event, Carter cried.

When it was over, Lisa told me to gather as many of the purple balloons as possible and bring them with us so Carter could enjoy them at home. I thought that was a terrible idea, but I started to collect the balloons. I knew I wouldn't be able to just hold onto handfuls of strings; they'd float away if I moved a finger. But I wanted to follow Lisa's orders to the extent I could and transport as many balloons as possible. I tried to recall everything I'd learned working at summer camp and spent ten minutes doing some senior Scout badge loom weaving magic to loop hundreds of purple balloon string ends together. I got them situated on my forearms in multiple sections, tied up securely for traveling, and this is how I left the theater, carried along by an entire nervous system of purple helium above me.

I bobbed along Central Park West under the cloud of swaying balloons, following Lisa more by intuition than ability to see. Somehow I got myself across the street at 81st. We stood in front of the American Museum of Natural History to wait for our driver. As we were standing there, a crowd of kids and adults in costumes started pouring from the entrance.

Lisa waved her hand at me through blobs of purple. "Look at all the kids! Why don't you give them some balloons?"

I did not like this idea. The balloons were now firmly attached to my body. But I said "Sure," and unsteadily approached the museum steps. Before I could get situated and detach the balloons for distribution, Lisa yelled, "Hey everybody! Come on over! Take some balloons!"

The crowd of New Yorkers who'd just been offered something for free looked over in one movement, then swarmed. Pirates, vampires, and sexy bumblebees jostled me from all sides, grabbing for the giveaway. Short kids ducked in at knee level to pull at strings. Parents appeared in between balloon clusters and didn't hesitate to use necessary force. They tugged from all directions, shoving each other in full Black Friday mode and jerking my body every which way. The balloon strings cut into my forearms as people snapped them loose from the intricate knotwork. Somewhere beyond the stampede I heard Lisa yelling. "Don't worry about it, come on! The car's here!" It was beyond my control. I closed my eyes and let my body bounce around as if I were in a trust fall circle at a leadership retreat.

The crowd finally finished with me, like a birthday party full of six-year-olds who've beat a pinata to death. Lisa motioned at me to hurry up.

With the ripped ends of strings dangling from my body and a few remaining balloons, I shuffled to the car. My witch's hat was trampled.

A few months later, I gave Lisa two weeks' notice. A long-term substitute teaching position had opened at the Y where I used to work. Lisa was not happy. She didn't have a job or any responsibilities besides managing us household staff: I resisted my guilt.

I started my first preschool classroom teaching job. I already knew my boss, Susan. At the end of my second week, Susan and I chatted as she helped me arrange picture books on the shelf. She was happy I was there; I was happy to be there; I was getting the hang of the routine. All was well.

"You know …" Susan said delicately. "She called me."

My hand froze on *Click Clack Moo*. "Who?"

"The woman you worked for."

Lisa had tracked down the number to the Y nursery school, gotten Susan on the line, and told her, "You really shouldn't hire Martha. She's not very good with my son, but I'm stuck … I need to keep her. You shouldn't hire her." Later, she'd called again and left a message on the machine: "Don't tell anyone about our conversation earlier … it's confidential."

Lisa once told me how she liked to steal tiny silver jam spoons from restaurants so Carter could use them at home. A friend had asked her how she could sleep at night, and she'd laughed, "I sleep just fine!"

I recently did some googling to see what happened to the family. Carter's now a teenage ski racer and amateur astronomer. It looks like they've run with his interest in stargazing by buying their way onto official scientific expeditions around the world, including an Antarctic solar eclipse viewing that was live streamed for NASA. Lisa was there, listed as a "citizen scientist."

It Went Out the Window

I HAD TO DRIVE TO a catering shift in the suburbs, and my uniform shirt wasn't ready. I'd thrown it in the wash after coming in from work the night before, but I didn't wake up in time to run it all the way through the dryer. Today's wedding was an hour commute. I figured I'd hang the damp shirt up in the car and it would finish drying on the way.

I had only one black shirt, and I washed it after every shift. Show me a server whose uniform comes out of an event spotless, and I'll show you someone who hid in the alley and chain-smoked while we loaded the truck at the end of the night. The rest of us are covered in chocolate ganache and trash juice like a low-seeded industry paintball team. It's a deterioration from the start of the evening, when we debut ourselves ironed and sheeny in the ballroom, pouring chestnut soup in teams of two for the Busby Berkeley-level opening number. Every cuff is fastened. We're fluttering at the judges.

How you look in catering is the most important part of the job. The dress code for my company was tailored black pants, black socks, black no-slip shoes, slim-fit long-sleeved black button-down shirt, and fitted black vest with decorative buckle in back. Have everything in place, and for God's sake, be smooth and tucked.

Uniforms are important. If you aren't in uniform, someone might accidentally get into a conversation with you, and then they've added you to their LinkedIn before they realize you're the Help. Then everyone feels hoodwinked, and the host gets mad. Servers need to be designated so they can be invisible, not to be addressed except when someone needs to point out that you're pouring wine wrong. ("Hold it higher," said the gentleman, after he ruminated on the label for sixteen seconds and then nodded with resentment.) The less uniform you wear, the higher your status. Think about your doctor. She gets to express a little personality with a cardigan ("So cold in here!") and whisper-thin flats while the nurse taking your urine has to wear scrubs and clodhoppers.

The uniform must be fresh, pressed, free of lint, smart and crisp in the manner of a British boarding school youth. The rest of yourself has to look on point, too. That means you must go into the bathroom with everyone else before a shift starts, line up in front of the mirror, and apply eyeliner with a heavy hand. The longer you've worked in catering, the more eyeliner you have to wear.

How you look has a direct impact on the dollars you earn. A notable Philadelphia designer once booked us for a holiday party and stipulated she wanted only good-looking servers, no uglies. (Guess who got put on the shift? Yeah, the call came in at the last minute, but did I get to trot out from bullpen to mound? You know it. I've updated my resume.)

Today, every part of me was ready except for the shirt. I prepared hair and face and dressed in my black pants, black socks, black shoes, and a skimpy black tank for the car. I tucked my folded-up vest (polyvinyl chloride; non-wrinkle) in my bag, on top of empty Tupperwares for taking leftover food home. I put my half-dry shirt on a white plastic hanger and hung it on the hook above the passenger seat window.

It was a glorious spring day. I got an iced coffee, got my Honda Fit onto the turnpike (the Kia had by that point been totaled, thank you for asking), and settled into the day's driving persona. This was not a day to be Multitasker (one hand peeling hard-boiled egg; applying lotion to calves) or Phone Conferencer ("Hang on, I gotta merge"). Today was a day to be Star of Soundtrack Montage. Caffeinated up, sunglasses on, flying down 276. *Got to Be Real, Ain't No Mountain High Enough, R-E-S-P-E-C-T.*

I looked over at my shirt, bouncing on the hanger. Would it dry in time? If I rolled the windows down, the draft would help it dry faster, right?

I lowered all four windows to get the air circulating. The wind rushed in and the shirt danced on the hanger to *Heatwave.* Its long sleeves whipped and snapped. Whee! I was so alive!

A gust of wind grabbed the shirt and sucked it off the hanger and out the open window.

The seconds stretched in slow motion. Closed captions rolled across my mind's eye. *This thing is happening. Is this thing happening? I don't want this thing to happen. This thing just happened.*

No. It can't! I needed my shirt. I had to get my shirt. I could stop the car, pull onto the shoulder, and run across the highway to retrieve it. I could hold my hand up like those Toad Detour volunteers who shepherd toads through high traffic areas during mating season.

In the split second I considered pulling over, I looked in the rearview mirror. The shirt floated delicately up on the breeze like Forrest Gump's feather, did a confident double axel and then gave up on life. It plummeted to the road surface and a tractor trailer ran over it. One sleeve wafted in a last gasp, then was done.

I was still driving at full speed. It was too late. The shirt was gone.

I slammed the volume button. I needed to think. What to do? Who else had seen? What if the other cars thought I did it on purpose? Some public radio donor would write down my tag number and report me for littering. What if they posted my details?

Dear Driver,

I am a third-grade student at Wickenburg Elementary. My class is learning how to write letters. You should not throw trash onto the highway. Our Earth needs love not litter. When I am a grownup, I will not throw trash out of my car. Sincerely, Piper Elizabeth Finnerty, age 8

I was going to be canceled. How could I have let this happen? I was usually so careful about things in the front seat. I never left my wallet exposed in case a cyclist reached in the open window at a stoplight, did a Nelson Muntz "HA-HA!" and pedaled off.

Now my shirt was gone, crumpled, abandoned after trusting me to care for it. Life is so cold. A relationship can be cut off, just like that. A montage of the life of the shirt flashed before my eyes: buying it at Goodwill; watching friendships develop with the other clothes in the laundry puddle holding pattern on the floor during the week; taking it out of the wash that morning.

Now I was showing up for my shift without my uniform shirt.

What would they do? Would they keep me in the kitchen all night? The last time I pitched in and sliced some limes, Chef Danny got a concerned look and took the knife away. If they kept me off the floor, we'd be short a server, and everyone would be annoyed. This work is about the collective. If you don't pull your weight on the dining room floor, you don't earn the privilege of tearing into the leftover cheese board after cocktail hour. It's clear who slacks and who doesn't. If you don't fall in, your cheese is unearned and everyone knows it.

I thought of the other staffers who wheeled in suitcases to every shift, ready with tackle boxes full of lip gloss, hairspray, needle and thread, lint roller, scotch tape to get the lint where the roller doesn't reach, breath freshener strips that melt on the tongue, aspirin, wet wipes, and unopened packets of Kleenex. They were ready to hole up in a bomb shelter with bottled water, protein bars, and packets of nuts. I was going to show up without my shirt.

Well, I was going to tell the truth. I refused to entertain the thought of saying I forgot my uniform because I *didn't*! I might be someone who rolled down the window going seventy on a blustery day with a five-ounce piece of fabric dangling by an air tunnel, but I was not someone who was UNPREPARED!

I arrived at the venue (two-story barn; mason jars) and went straight to my boss Ed, who was still in his pre-event t-shirt as the team set up tables. His suit would be hanging up in the kitchen, covered in plastic, with a color-coordinated tie unspooled against it. "Ed," I said. "I have a problem."

Ed's whole job as captain was to troubleshoot. His purpose was to be ready with a smile when a rookie server spilled red wine onto someone's dress: materializing with a napkin dipped in club soda, dabbing at a stranger's bosom with confidence.

Ed held up a finger as he finished counting place settings, then gestured for me to continue.

"My shirt went out the window on the highway," I said.

Ed was such a ninja at his job that he allowed himself only a third of a second to chuckle as he issued place cards around the table. When he was finished, he looked at me, raised a finger and said, "I have an idea."

I followed him to the kitchen. "You have your vest?" he asked. I nodded. "Take my shirt, wear it under your vest," he said.

He removed his long-sleeved tee. Ed was bigger than me, with much longer arms. The shirt had faded from black to pencil-smudge gray after so many washes and had the company logo on the chest. It was a shirt you'd sleep in at best.

He handed me his shirt and grabbed his pink button-down to dress himself.

I went into the barn bathroom on the lower level and put Ed's shirt over my tank, with my vest on top. I looked in the mirror. The shirt was enormous. The logo peeked out from under the vest panel and the sleeves billowed like a Shakespearean fool. I rolled the cuffs a few times. It only made the billowing more pronounced. I'm no student of fashion, but I believe the technical term is *bishop sleeve*. I looked like a struggling magician slash comedian at a Los Angeles street carnival.

All night I swashbuckled around the room with my big sleeves, serving appetizers, clearing empties. The sleeves jostled champagne glasses and drooped in someone's mashed potatoes. Bits of food from dirty plate stacks hitchhiked onto the excess fabric. *"Hey guys, get on! There's room in the back!"*

I was sure a guest would complain about how terrible I looked or say within earshot, "Who is that hand-me-down buccaneer pouring the wine?" Someone might accuse me of trespassing, a reverse wedding crasher who stopped by after a cosplay event but instead of dancing decided to clean up.

I envisioned the bride's mother collaring me on my way to the kitchen.

"Listen," she hisses. Her chunky gold bracelet shakes as she points at me. "You are going to have to stay in the back. We paid a lot of money for this, and you are bringing down the classy factor."

"But I need to clear your sea bass—"

"I'll do it myself!"

Next, the groom stops me in the stairwell, furious. "Is this some kind of joke?"

"What? No—"

"Yeah, I was a big Renaissance Faire guy for years. Headlined the Bawdy Poetry event. I left that life behind, okay? Who sent you? Was it the wench from Glassblowing?"

"No! I promise!"

Ed gestures from the doorway. "Martha, help me move the cake table onto the floor. It's almost time for the cutting."

"But I—"

"Go!"

I sneak across the dance floor. Everyone is jumping up and down to Shout! The bride accosts me just as I get to the cake. "We all know why you're here. Tell that wench to stay out of our lives!" She lunges. The groom throws a punch at Ed. We all fall into the cake, and it topples to the floor. The guests shout "a little bit louder now". My sleeves are covered in buttercream.

A drunk groomsman takes the microphone. "I'll be substituting for the best man tonight!" he yells. "Unfortunately he couldn't be here for the toast; he got in an accident on the turnpike when a shirt flew onto his windshield and caused a pile-up. Anyway, I have to tell you about what me and the bride got up to last night—"

The bride leaps toward him but is restrained by the maid of honor.

He continues. "Oh, and apparently the shirt was thrown out of a red Honda Fit, so if anyone—"

"I saw that car in the lot!" an uncle yells. "Slash the tires! KILL THE BEAST!" The crowd empties out of the barn.

"Hey." Another server pokes me. "Didn't your shirt go out the window?"

"You're done in this business!" Chef Danny yells at me from the floor, scooping lumps of frosting onto dessert plates as he tries to salvage the cake. "Go home! NO! You don't get any leftovers! Put your Tupperwares away!"

In the end, nobody seemed to notice. After we packed the truck, I took Ed's shirt off, tucked in my tank top, and brought the shirt back to Ed. "Worked out okay, didn't it?" he said, smiling.

I got a new shirt from the thrift store. It fit fine.

Dancing Down Pawn Shop Alley

My friend Chantal is the most fashionable person I know. She is so fashionable that she attended Meghan Markle and Prince Harry's wedding in an emerald green hat, but that's another story. This story is about when she gave me a Louis Vuitton laptop bag.

Chantal and I met when we were roommates in college. The most exciting thing about her wardrobe was that she and I wore the same size. I owned mostly thrift store items and allotted my work-study money for food, not going-out shirts. Chantal gave me her hand-me-downs at the rate she acquired new clothes, which was rapid. Once on her way to class she decided she didn't like her outfit and stopped in the Gap to buy a new sweater.

A few years after graduation, I was in a freelancing stage and desperate for cash. I started to go through everything I owned to see what I could peddle. I uncovered the silver men's watch an old roommate had given me when he'd moved out of our apartment, and a thrill came over me. "You could sell it," he'd suggested at the time. I'd totally forgotten about it. Now I set aside the watch, along with an iPod Nano an employer had given me last Christmas.

Around the same time that I was gathering these items, I saw Chantal. Before we parted ways, she handed me a bag of stuff she was getting rid of, as per tradition. I went through it. Some clothes I would wear, some I wouldn't, and at the bottom—a Louis Vuitton laptop bag.

I pulled it out. "Are you sure you don't want this?" I asked, my heart starting to beat fast.

"Take it," she said, waving her hand.

Make no mistake. Me carrying a Louis Vuitton bag would be a *What's wrong with this picture?* seek 'n' find. But you know what I could do with it, right?

The bag had to be worth hundreds of dollars. Maybe even a thousand! How could she just hand it over to me like that? I wanted to ask what it might be worth, but it felt like a delicate subject. Chantal was always getting rid of fancy items. This was no different. It was just a lucky break that this happened at a time when I needed it. I didn't know anything about designer stuff, but I knew that *Vogue* magazine was full of ads for Louis Vuitton luggage, and it was always carried by people on boats. People on boats have money. The logic was clear.

Maybe this could be my new thing. Maybe I could function fully as a resale queen, acquiring items and selling them, taking over the eBay economy and being my own boss. I could live by scrapping and hustling and this bag sale would prove it.

I stuffed the iPod, watch, and Louis Vuitton bag into a duffel and headed into Center City. I know it's not good to get ahead of yourself, but I was already planning what I would buy at Wawa when I had cash in my pocket.

A store on Market Street had a sign out front saying it bought used electronics. I went in and proudly showed the guy my iPod. It was free of cracks. In great shape!

He wasn't impressed. "I can give ya five dollars," he said, unenthusiastic.

I tried not to show how disappointed I was. He leaned on his elbows over the counter and looked me up and down, a little amused. "Ya new in town?"

I hesitated. Were we supposed to pretend we were in a 1940s movie? Should I play like I was a hard-boiled dame in a wool suit and hat, and say out of the side of my mouth, "Who's askin'?" Then he'd reply, "I got a fella who'll rent ya a room for a dime a week," and I would say as I lit up a long cigarette, "Thanks, but I'm a lady who can take care of herself."

Instead, I pulled the iPod back and muttered "Naw, thanks," transformed now into a Depression-era boy in overalls tromping around town holding out for a deal on his red wagon so he can buy his Ma some shoes.

It was a blow, but a minor blow. I had the watch, and of course the holy grail, the bag.

The watch had an etching on the back that said "Bulova." I wasn't sure if that was a top brand or not. But it looked like a nice watch. It looked like a watch worn by a man flying a single-propeller plane, neck scarf flapping behind him. A watch worn by a man with a strong jawline. It had the tiniest scratch on the face—no doubt there was a story to go with that, from a brush with death while climbing Machu Picchu. It probably would add to its value.

I headed for Jeweler's Row, a stretch of buy-and-sell stores along Chestnut Street. Maybe I was bringing in a watch that these store owners had been trying to find for years. They would probably fawn over me, bring me some champagne and petit fours, and have me sit in a shaggy faux fur chair. Maybe I could go into one store, get their offer, then go next door and pit them against each other. Then there would be a Street Fighter situation to determine the winner. I would watch from my chair, smiling and nodding.

I walked confidently into the first store and presented the watch. A guy fresh from the tanning bed with slicked-back hair said, "We don't buy those. Try across the street." Okay, too high-end for him. Understood. I marched across the street, and a little bell announced my entry into the carpeted shop.

A tiny woman who looked like she'd been working there for a hundred years emerged from the back and took out a jeweler's spyglass with a pirate vibe. She looked the watch over.

The longer she examined it, the more hope swelled inside me. I would use a hundred to pay my car insurance. The next hundred for my student loan. The last hundred ... cell phone bill and new jeans?

She removed her spyglass and looked at me sympathetically. "I hate to tell you this," she said. "But if somebody offers you five dollars, you better take it."

"Really?" I said graciously, hoping she'd elaborate or say, "Just kidding! Here's two hundred bucks." She sighed and pointed to the watch, saying, "Yeah, you can't get much for that." She seemed so truly sad it felt alarming. Was this the worst watch she had ever seen? Was this the final straw, and after being in the game for so long, she was going to quit after today?

I pretended that I understood, that naturally it made sense, and thanked her. I didn't understand. This watch had heavy links, for goodness' sake. What was wrong with this economy? Okay, well, it didn't matter. I still had the crown jewel—the Louis Vuitton.

I walked down the street to Buffalo Exchange, a resale shop full of racks of dresses, jackets and t-shirts. I took a number and went to sit and wait with other hopefuls in aluminum chairs.

I pulled the Louis bag out of my duffel and looked at it. My designer bag was clean, sturdy, and straight from Chantal's closet. What did my colleagues have, some Old Navy jeans? I started to feel cocky. I looked around at the other sellers, hoping to meet someone's eye so I could nod down at my bag and whisper meaningfully, *"Louis Vuitton."* Like a beauty pageant mom psyching out the other moms before the show as she applies hot pink lipstick to her five-year-old with a smug smile. *Three-time champion of Claiborne County; y'all might as well go home now.*

No one met my eye. They were all clutching stacks of club clothes and flannel shirts tight against their bodies and staring ahead. It was like waiting to go to Confession, with a palpable anxiety about dumping the results of our choices before a stranger and waiting for judgment.

I held Louis gently in front of me like the calm, professional, high-class salesperson I was. The counter guy called my number.

I walked up and put the bag down proudly, palms up: *You're welcome.* I waited for a gasp of approval: *Is that a real Louis Vuitton? Wow, it's in such good shape.*

Counter Guy started to examine the bag like he was giving a full physical to a small dog. He ran his finger all over the edges, tested its response to pressure; pushed both hands down on the bottom with eyebrows scrunching into a frown. He opened the flap, stuck his head inside and inhaled deeply. Then he flipped the whole thing over, hardened his mouth into a thin line, and pushed the bag toward me with two fingers.

He said, "This is fake. We don't take fake bags."

I blinked.

It couldn't be. The bag said Louis Vuitton. It looked like a Louis Vuitton. Who was I to question it? Surely ... surely Chantal wouldn't have a fake bag?

Counter Guy stared at me with pursed lips. I said, "No, my friend gave it to me. It's real."

He cleared his throat and took a deep breath. "It's not a real Louis Vuitton, you can tell because of the stitching right here."

"My friend got it and it's real," I repeated, as if I could convince him. My protest only drove him further. He started manhandling the imposter bag.

"The stitching isn't symmetrical over here, and it's too perfectly angled there—that's how you know it was machine made. This thread wouldn't be this color. It's not the right shade of yellow. See?" My mouth was open as if to argue, but he kept going. "Look at the stamp on the inside. The letters here are too far apart. And the copyright sign is shifted too far from the center line between letters V and U here."

Counter Guy had a new look in his eye now: the fire of conviction. He had been waiting his whole life for this moment. All the editions of *Harper's Bazaar* he studied behind his algebra textbooks, all the long hours spent separating the wheat from the chaff at this godforsaken retail job for monsters like me who wouldn't know a Marc Jacobs from a Coach from a goddamn Abercrombie and Fitch.

"Also, the stitching on the stamp here is uneven. That's how you know it's fake." A lawyer giving his final summation, knowing he won his case against the blockhead who chose to self-represent. He pushed the bag toward me again and concluded, "We don't take fake bags."

Unable to accept it, I gripped the counter with stiff fingers. How could Chantal have had a fake bag? Did she know it was fake? My world was spinning. Could nothing be counted on in this life? Did my parents love me? Did God exist? "It's real ... it's real," I whispered, almost to convince myself. Wildly I thought back to a short story we read in seventh grade called *The Necklace* where some poor woman borrows jewelry, loses it, and spends her whole life repaying for its replacement only to find out the original gemstones were nothing but paste. I'd been duped. Tears sprung to the corners of my eyes. I *couldn't* walk out of here with no money.

Seeing that I wasn't moving, Counter Guy folded his arms and glared. He said, "Ma'am ..." —the final blow— "... we cannot take this." He picked up a container of Purell next to the register and doused his fingers. Then he called the next number.

The other beauty pageant moms watched as I lifted the bag off the counter and carried it out of the store into the bright light of day. *Why can't we just say it's a real Louis Vuitton?* I wanted to shout. What was the difference? Who would know?

I drove home with the duffel still holding the iPod Nano, the watch, and the Louis Vuitton bag. When I passed Wawa, I didn't look.

A few months later, I casually mentioned it to Chantal. "Oh yeah," she said, "of course it was fake." She laughed. "Did you think I would have given it to you if it was real?"

I gave the bag away to a charity thrift shop. They were happy to take it.

I'm Still Afraid of Matches

I NEVER WAS A SMOKER. I like the smell of cigarettes, though. It's nostalgia. I worked at overnight camp in the Pennsylvania woods during college summers, and everybody smoked. Counselors snuck cigarettes on back porches while lightning bugs blinked in the trees, and down by the boat dock at sunset. Officially, smoking was allowed only in the staff lounge, which was full of old porch furniture and was next to the flagpole field, in full view of the campers. Clauses in the staff handbook read: *The Camp Director will beat any and all staff if there is evidence of smoking outside the staff lounge* and *Staff members under the age of 18 may smoke only with written permission from a parent or guardian.*

It was the early 2000s. Things were different. It was pretty much anything goes as long as the kids survived.

Twenty-four hours a day, six days a week, we lived with campers in cabins painted red, the porches strung with wet bathing suits and beach towels. We yelled at our kids to take showers and stop dancing naked, and slept on cracked vinyl mattresses in metal bunk beds with sagging springs.

Cool air and cricket song floated through the screened windows at night. Daddy-long-legs raced through the showers and moths held family reunions around the porch lights. On rainy days, we sat on the back porch and watched the rain fall through the trees, and our kids played cards and made messes. Sometimes we leaned into it and got our campers in bathing suits, splashing in puddles and washing hair under the drainpipe downpour. One wet summer, a mudslide developed down the boys' side field. Everybody rushed over to take turns sailing through the slime, coming up caked in mud and running back to the top to do it again.

Most days, we swam in the pool and took our groups to Sports and Arts and Crafts. We supervised campers at the climbing wall and on long creek walks. We watched the tree leaves breathing in the breeze down at the lake and the sunlight filtering through onto the glassy surface of the water. The lake was disgusting, so staff constantly tried to push each other off the boat dock. If you were a victim, your bathing suit stunk for the rest of the week. Water snakes went after you, too. I got a bite on my ankle and the tooth marks took days to fade.

Before a few hours off each night, we had the Evening Colors flagpole ceremony and a special camp-wide Evening Activity that went with the week's theme. Halloween week we played Bonkers. Counselors painted themselves like clowns, put on tie-dyed t-shirts, and pummeled kids with socks full of flour. For Christmas week, the local fire company pumped the grass full of eye-burning firefighting foam and three hundred people dove into the "snow" for a free-for-all. There were always a lot of injuries from that one.

Counselor Roundup, a jailbreak game, was during Wild West Week. It was the last week of the summer, right when things started going off the rails. Counselors in cowboy hats hid in bushes or hay wagons. Other staff, campers cheering behind them, dragged out the cowboys, signaled the kids to pile on, got them into a safe hold and escorted them to the jail. It wasn't gentle.

It was a bit like Braveheart, which we played during staff training week. The goal of Braveheart was to run from one end of the soccer field to the other, while the person who was "it" tried to tackle runners to the ground. If you hit the ground, you also became "it," so the squad of tacklers increased each round until everyone had been brought down. The first year, it was pouring rain, and fifty of us went for broke in the mud. People got hurt every year, banging heads, twisting ankles.

Braveheart was invented by Dave. He was one of the admin team, the supervisors in their early twenties who oversaw us counselors ranging in age from sixteen to twenty-three. Dave was Head Counselor. He was from Scotland and called bathing suits "swimming costumes" and sneakers "trainers." Dave had an air of mystery I couldn't crack. He seemed quite serious about everything and I rarely saw him smile, but then he'd come out of nowhere with a dirty joke or prank. He seemed to be the most responsible person on camp, yet at the same time, the least mature. It was a fascinating combination.

During staff training week we sat in a circle of fifty stackable metal chairs in the wood-cabin meeting hall cooled by industrial fans. Along with "Dave's Daily Fun and Games" icebreakers, Dave led the sessions working our way through the staff handbook, which he had written. It was full of Easter eggs; I think to keep himself amused but also as a reward for anyone who bothered to pay attention all the way through.

The handbook warned us of overheating: *THE HEAT WILL KILL YOU.* It talked about thunderstorm safety: *Having our campers struck by lightning would really suck and it would make us look a little bad.* There was a section titled *What Lurks in the Trees* that included skunks (*For you who don't know what they look like, they look like stocky cats that have been tumble dried*) and tick removal (*Don't be macho... you can either take it like a man or use some sort of sting-eez.*)

Dave's handbook outlined guidance on child discipline (*The fact that you harbor thoughts of murder from time to time is quite normal and even healthy*) and camp relationships (*You have to remember that the kids emulate you and if you're flirting heavily with each other right in front of little Fitzroy, well then little Fitzroy thinks that it's okay to flirt outrageously with any girl he fancies. Then little Amber goes home and tells mom that Fitzroy is saying all sorts of weird things to her like "I saw you naked!" So please control your hormones in this regard so that kids can stay kids a wee bit longer.)*

We had orange plastic lock boxes stacked against the walls in the downstairs office to keep valuables. One evening I went into the office to sign out. Dave, on duty that night, had built a fort out of the lock boxes and was patrolling from behind the wall wearing a Davy Crockett coonskin hat. Other evenings, he stretched out on the sagging couch on the admin cabin's front porch. There he took pen and paper and wrote letters for Amnesty International to free political prisoners. Occasionally when visiting to see how we were getting on with our kids, he'd drop some breadcrumbs about his life. He had put himself through university in Scotland playing pro rugby while getting his degree in religious studies with a focus on feminism. He had worked as a Santa Claus and bus tour guide in Scotland. He once offered conspiratorially, "I have a special surprise for Colors. I'm wearing my short shorts." He showed up to the field in hi-cut scrum shorts with less coverage than most Speedos.

Dave often filled in at the infirmary. It was a struggle to keep a camp nurse for the whole summer, and the ones we managed to get came only in the daytime. So every night after Evening Activity Dave handled meds.

My time at camp coincided with the surge in children being pre-scribed medication for ADHD. Half the campers were taking Ritalin, and on the busiest weeks, ninety kids needed medication before bed. It was the last responsibility of the evening for counselors not on night duty, so after dismissal from the Colors field they rushed their campers down the hill in a take-no-prisoners gallop to be first in line at the infirmary. Dave, alone behind the plastic table in the carpeted cinderblock hall, called out the order of distribution in a pharmaceutical Hunger Games. Untrained beyond First Aid, he followed dozens of different requirements for the psychotropics and tranquilizers: some pills had to be broken in half, some taken with water, some without, and everything documented on paper. Occasionally a five-year-old who wasn't prescribed anything would tag along with his age group and say, "I want medicine." Dave would give him a teaspoon of water and send him on his way.

Staff-to-camper ratios weren't a thing. After dinner, counselors blew off steam playing soccer. The ones who weren't playing were watching, which left five staff assigned to supervise two hundred kids having free time. There were no cell phones back then, just a pay phone outside the meeting hall, and we had a number of international staff on summer work visas. Every so often the camp director blared over the PA system: "German Tom, please come to the office; you have a phone call." (Tom from America was called American Tom and Tom from Germany was called German Tom, even after American Tom was fired. An average of five staff per summer got the sack, plus those lost to legitimate injuries or the underperformers who exaggerated a knee twinge midway through the season as an excuse to use the golf cart.) German Tom, or Anna from Poland, or Matt from Wales, would run up to the office, excited to talk to someone from home for an hour in the air-conditioned office. Their partner was left with twenty kids at the boat dock. Of course, the American counselors also skipped out for long smoke breaks, naps, or hanging out with the cabin of someone they had a crush on.

I don't want to give the impression that we didn't take our job seriously. Everyone took a lot of pride in being a good camp counselor. It was cool to be good. Staff were noticed and admired when they managed campers effectively or pulled off something impressive for the theme days and traditions. Everyone talked about who had won Best Counselor, Best Skits, and Hardest Worker the previous year. (There were also awards for Best Legs and Nicest Bum.) That first year, I was as eager as everyone else to be a great counselor, and just as importantly, to be seen as one.

Monday morning of Olympic Week, Dave approached me. He had a way of striding along with purpose, head cocked to one side. I was leading my group across camp in pajama pants, flip-flops and white wife beater, drinking coffee from the cafeteria out of a paper Dart Solo cup, the kind with the jazzy turquoise and purple graphic. "Martha," Dave said, stopping and putting hands on hips. He was wearing his "Drink or Die" t-shirt (it meant alcohol, but he maintained that it was about hydration.) "Would you like to carry the torch for Opening Ceremonies tonight?"

Of course I said yes. It felt like a serious initiation to be given the honor only four weeks into my camp experience. There were lots of opportunities to be in the spotlight: veteran staff members sang acoustic Indigo Girls covers at the weekly Staff Show or led the "Your Mama Wears Army Boots" cheer at the campfire; I hadn't put myself out there for anything yet. Now Dave was asking me, specifically, to do something important.

Dave told me my job would be to receive the torch handoff from the first runner and run it to the Colors field for the ceremonial lighting. The whole camp would be there, ready for the parade of flags from their chosen nations.

The other torch runner was Jonathan from Archery. Jonathan was a very nice priest-in-training. The camp was run by the Archdiocese; they sometimes sent a seminarian to work the summers. They had recently had a bad track record of seminarians coming to camp, falling in love, and abandoning the priesthood, so it was a risk, but we needed an Archery instructor. For a while the diocese also sent us the same alcoholic priest every year to hang out for a week. The guy had great hair but he was always a bit drunk.

Jonathan had a real sense of duty. He always pitched in with whatever was needed, and he helped set up for Mass. He was quiet, with surprising bursts of enthusiasm during cheers or skits. Jonathan had a side part, and hated whenever anyone touched his hair. Of course the guys made a game out of trying to touch it. So he took to wearing a hat.

That night, everyone proceeded to the Colors field with their flags, and I went to stand at the torch hand-off spot near the basketball courts. I had my sneakers on. I was ready. The bullhorn sounded, "Chariots of Fire" started playing from the speakers, and everyone turned to look in my direction.

I watched for Jonathan from Archery, and he appeared from behind the ten-foot team-building wall at the edge of the woods, running toward me at a frantic pace, carrying the—

Oh.

When Dave said, "Olympic torch," I envisioned a neat paper towel tube, with some tissue paper glued to the top in alternating layers of yellow, orange and red. He hadn't explained in detail; I filled in the gaps. Gold glitter, maybe, for effect.

Jonathan was not carrying a paper towel tube. It was a huge tree branch that had been wrapped in a rag secured with rubber bands, doused in gasoline, and lit on fire. The ball of flame coming toward me was two feet in diameter.

The closer Jonathan from Archery got to me, the more scared I got. The torch was blazing and hot and spitting sparks like a piece of furniture from Satan's living room. Jonathan was moving at top speed, looking extremely uncomfortable but determined. He arrived red-faced at my spot and held the torch out, sweat dripping from his head. "Take it!" he said with urgency. "Take it!"

I hesitated. How could I possibly transport this much fire? Jonathan was in agony, about to melt. Smoke choked the air between us. "Take it!" he said again.

I had to do it. I reached through the hot smoke for the bottom of the stick, the part that wasn't on fire. I thought it would make the most sense to hold the flame as far away from me as possible, lengthwise like a tennis player doing a forehand. The flame instantly shot down the gasoline-soaked stick and hit my hand. My hand was on fire. I threw the blazing branch down into the dry grass.

I stared at my blackened hand. The parched July field started to smoke and crackle at our feet. Three hundred campers and staff watched and waited. Jonathan from Archery did not have time for this.

Jonathan got a look of cold steel in his eyes like he was about to deliver a baby and dove into the ball of fire in the grass. He grabbed the torch and took off in a wild sprint for the Colors field. You couldn't tell where the fire ended and Jonathan from Archery began; it was one huge ball of light with sparks trailing behind like fireworks. The field of campers pulled a Red Sea and Jonathan ran through the middle, bolted up the ladder at the front, and into the silver bowl at the top dropped the burning Olympic torch.

Horns blew and the presentation of flags began. I stood alone at the torch handoff spot, looking toward the field, then at my hand. It was stinging with pain. Dave loped over.

"What happened?" he asked in his non-judgmental Scottish accent. I told him. He inspected my hand and explained that you should always hold a stick upright if it's on fire. "Go to the infirmary," he said. "I'll be there in a moment."

I could see the sun setting through the window as I sat on the metal folding chair in the infirmary next to Jonathan. He was completely scorched. All the hair had burned off both his arms. He sat there calmly, without speaking. He seemed to be in a meditative state.

Dave told me to run my hand under lukewarm water while he tended to Jonathan.

"You guys were on fire and you didn't let go," Dave said. "Why did you not let go?"

Jonathan said nothing as Dave bandaged him up. He had saved Opening Ceremonies. He'd done his duty.

I didn't say anything either. Because, you'll remember, I did let go.

It was my turn. Dave wrapped my hand in a white bandage and looked back and forth from Jonathan's arms to my hand. "I don't know why the fuck we do this shit," he said. "This is so stupid."

Two cabins' worth of shouting kids arrived at the door, fighting to get in first as the counselors behind them yelled, "Hurry up and go to the front!"

It was time for evening meds. I thanked Dave and headed across the field to my cabin. It was dark now, and cicadas were loud in the trees. I had the happy, satisfied feeling you always got at camp at nighttime. My bandage was as thick as a cast, and I lifted my arm up and down to feel the weight of it. I don't know. I felt kind of proud.

Years later I asked Dave how he decided who to pick for things like carrying the Olympic torch. "Well," he told me, "my role was risk and stupidity mitigation. We would have these stupid plans, and then I would decide who wasn't going to do something foolish and mess it up."

Jonathan from Archery won Most Willing to Volunteer that year and was runner-up for Most Enthusiastic. Dave won Most Likely to Rule the World and Best Legs. The next year for Opening Ceremonies, they didn't use a stick-and-rag situation. Eddie from England carried a tiki torch, and he walked instead of ran. It didn't have the same zazz.

To IRS, With Love

November 5th

Dear IRS,

Thank you for your letter dated November 1st. It's nice to hear from you!

I can't thank you enough for alerting me to the error in my 2019 tax filing. How mortifying! I assure you it wasn't personal. Our longstanding bond ranks you as one of my favorite government agencies and I value our relationship. I hope I didn't cause any offense. As always, I admire your work!

Not to make excuses, but I do want to explain myself. No longer wanting to trade a handsome sum for meddling questions from the H&R Block guy, I put on a blazer and a *Her Money* podcast and sat down to do my taxes myself. You of all people know how complicated it can be for freelancers, but I figured if I could help a fifth grader with New Math, I can interpret these forms. I can only blame all the motivational speakers who told me I could do anything and express my gratitude that you checked my numbers. We're nothing without our editors, right?

An audit will be a chance to Marie Kondo—shake the dust bunnies off. I'm grateful for the opportunity!

I'd love to talk things through on the phone and sort this out. In the meantime, know that your letter is hanging proudly on the fridge.

Sincerely,
Martha

November 10th

Dear IRS,

It's occurred to me what an honor it is to have been chosen for an audit. I know not everyone gets this kind of attention, and it's a special thing. I've taken to carrying your documents with me everywhere. Looking them over makes me feel that in this great big world, I matter. Thank you for that.

Today while in line at the pharmacy, I re-read the Taxpayer Bill of Rights. Your words are reassuring, especially "If we inquire about your return or select it for examination, it does not suggest that you are dishonest." I was relieved to see that.

The section about talking to outside sources such as "newspaper, public records, and individuals" does give me pause. Do you mind not mentioning anything to my mom? I appreciate it.

Your Friend,
Martha

November 20th

Dear IRS,

I've been trying to reach you by phone. It's tricky to get through! I explained to the automated voice that I had received a personal letter and you were expecting my call, but it seems I couldn't be connected to you directly. I don't want you to think I'm ignoring you. Give me a shout—you have my number.

In other news, my ficus plant is doing so well, he graduated to a new pot! I enclosed a photo. Do you have a green thumb?

Talk soon,
Martha

December 3rd

Dear IRS,

Did you catch me visiting your website last night? I thought that might be a better way to reach you. When I logged in, it said I didn't owe anything, even though your letter mentioned quite a high number. I'm sure it's a matter of wires getting crossed! I can imagine the intra-office pranking that goes on, and your cubemate trying to keep you from reaching this month's goals by fudging the data! Either way, I'm eager to get things cleared up. Our relationship is important to me, and I think about you often.

Yours,
Martha

December 31st

Dear IRS,

I was overjoyed to get your mail dated December 27th, but to be honest it was a disappointment to find twenty pages of documents instead of the expected holiday photo card. Did you get my Christmas newsletter?

I'm sorry you had to work over the holidays!

Mail correspondence can feel so distant. I'd love to meet up in person to dive in and correct this issue together! I adore Washington D.C.—short buildings; expensive sandwiches. We could make a day of it! I have been wanting to see Julia Child's kitchen at the American History Museum.

We can sort everything out while we stroll, and I really want to get to know you better, too. How did your career path unfold? Did you always want to be the IRS? Which Hogwarts house are you?

I think we have something special, and I want to KIG – keep it going.

Xo,
Martha

January 14th

Dear IRS,

I know it's late. I can't sleep. I've listened to the "Relaxing Ocean Waves" meditation and *Moby-Dick* on audiobook, and nothing's working. I keep going over our last communication in my head.

Your actions and words—they don't always line up. Sometimes it seems like you don't want this, yet you keep coming back. Are you trying to make me prove myself? I get it—we've all been let down before. Don't you think I understand that? I'm here for this, IRS. I'm all in. The question is, are you?

I love you,
Martha

January 15th

Dear IRS,

I woke up today with the breakthrough that this isn't a matter of He's Just Not That Into You— we're simply speaking different love languages. I'm looking for Quality Time, while you want Gifts.

I know a good couples therapist—would you like me to set something up?

Love never fails,
Martha

February 17th

Dear IRS,

You've been pretty quiet—are you doing all right? These winter blues can get to all of us.

You have my number—just text.

xoxo,
Martha

February 24th

Dear IRS,

I was overjoyed to get your recent letter dated February 22nd! Thank goodness you are well. I was beginning to get worried.

I notice there are only four pages, and there's reference to a plan that I wasn't consulted on. I'm eager to problem-solve as well, but I'd prefer some input to the conversation? Remember, it's me and you against the problem—not me against you. Relationships are about compromise, right?

Do you want to get together this week to hammer it out? I could make a lasagna.

Kisses,
Martha

March 1st

Dear IRS,

I don't mean to be a downer, but I'm not in the best frame of mind today. Everyone around me is getting excited for tax season, and we still haven't resolved our spat.

I usually love this time of year. I got the bin of decorations down from the attic, but the 1099 garlands are still sitting in a pile on the floor, next to the cardboard calculators I always scotch-tape to the bay window. I don't have the heart.

I didn't even send out cards this year. How can I? I feel like an imposter, going around and wishing people a happy holiday season, when underneath it all, we're at odds. I want to celebrate, too. I want to wear a sticker that says, "I Did My Taxes." But I can't.

To top it off, Netflix is showing one Tax Season special after another, and I can't stop myself. It's a way to press the bruise.

> Thinking of you,
> Martha

March 4th

Dear IRS,

For finding me among a whole universe of potential people ... thank you.

For recognizing my uniqueness and making me feel like the only girl in the world ... thank you.

For never forgetting me ... thank you.

For always being there ... thank you.

> Love always,
> Martha

March 5th

Dear IRS,

You know what? I'm getting tired of this. I give you everything, show you vulnerability, and you don't even have the decency to respond? And when you do, it's a template letter? Don't think I didn't notice that your paperwork has been arriving from all different locations. Holtsville, NY; Cincinnati; Austin?! Why are you traveling so much? Are you the Tinder Swindler? How many people are you even corresponding with? Is it too much to expect a little personal attention? You take, and take, and take, and never give.

I'm done.
Martha

March 6th

Dear IRS,

I'm really embarrassed about my last message. I had a long day and too much Chex Mix. Please, pretend it never happened. When you want to talk, I'm here.

I love you,
Martha

March 14th

Dear IRS,

It's quiet here at the seaside in the wintertime. Nice to get away from the city noise. The beach is empty, and I've been taking long walks, collecting sea pebbles and broken shells from the cold sand. I've been thinking about you a lot. Do you ever get the chance to take a break and look out over the water? To watch the waves tumbling toward you, and contemplate the never-ending passage of time? I'm reminded of T.S. Eliot: "I have heard the mermaids singing, each to each … I do not think they will sing to me."

They say life is a spiraling curriculum, like the channeled whelk shell I tucked into my canvas bag this morning. We travel along its rounded edges, destined to repeat the same mistakes until we learn from them. I'm ready to fix my past mistakes, IRS. I hope you'll let me.

Love,
Your Martha

March 16th

Dear IRS,

Thank you for giving me the opportunity to find my voice. This is the last time you will be hearing from me. Love is a two-way street, and I'm strong enough now to read the road signs.

I've tried, IRS. My money could have been yours. I wanted nothing more than to sit together in a buttery-leather booth, hold hands over a plate of silver dollar pancakes, and sign on the dotted line. But I'm not waiting around. I've got my water shoes on, and I can paddle my own canoe. Don't try to find me.

Liberté,
Martha J. Cooney

The Priest and the Heist

I BECAME FRIENDS WITH MICHELLE sophomore year of high school. That was the year she got a black eye when she took on three girls on the school bus after they called her a Japanese bitch. She got suspended. Our religion teacher started calling her Rocky.

Michelle was someone who got stuff done. She saw an efficient way around our perpetual cycle of rolling up our gray plaid uniform skirts, being yelled at by the Library Nun to unroll them and rolling them back up again: she got her mom to hem her skirt up short. She wore big Aaliyah hoops and was buddies with the one true punk in our grade who safety-pinned fabric scraps of band logos on his denim jacket. Michelle worked as a promoter and gave out flyers and stickers for the first-ever Philly nightlife website. People got pink slips for putting those stickers on their lockers, but somehow it never got traced back to her.

I was in a lot of after school clubs and so was Michelle, so we waited together in the evenings for the SEPTA bus from school in the burbs back home to northeast Philly. She was in the community service club with me, and senior year we both worked on the Christmas toy drive.

I was president of the service club. We had to do forty hours of community service to graduate; people came to me to hook them up. I had to sign off on their hours and everything. It beefed up my social currency, and I can't say I didn't enjoy the power. Nobody bothered with me in high school unless they needed something: geometry help; copying Spanish homework; joining my group for English presentations because I turned oral reports into full-scale productions with mixtape soundtrack and a guaranteed A. Being used was better than being ignored. You know what I got voted senior year? Most Helpful. Every high school kid's ambition, being voted Most Helpful.

I would have run the service club on my own out of the maintenance closet, with kids approaching me Godfather style as I swiveled around from behind a desk, pulled out a big binder, and made them sweat while I decided assignments. Unfortunately, we were required to have faculty advisors. So I had to manage Mrs. Murphy from Guidance, and Father Jugenheimer.

Jugenheimer was an angry priest who taught senior religion. He had a way of gliding along the hallways, his lower body strolling in a casual gait, his upper body in a shoulder hunch and chin-up surveillance. He rolled in and out of classrooms like a real-life Snape in clerical black. Jugie did not tolerate any discussion of morality except to reiterate the official church stance.

"How do we know God is real?" Michelle asked him.

"You're being inappropriate, Miss Freeman," he said, putting down his paper cup filled with ice and diet Coke from the cafeteria soda fountain. Jugie went full body when he got angry, and he needed his arms free so he could flail.

"Why does the church tell us to vote for Bush?" I attempted on a periodic basis. I'd spent that summer protesting the Republican National Convention and reading Howard Zinn, Martin Luther King Jr., Dorothy Day. Jugie was not there for it.

"That is ENOUGH, Miss Cooney!" he raged every time my hand went up. His black hair puffed out on the sides of his reddening face. The yelling was worth it to see the performance.

Jugenheimer and Mrs. Murphy weren't fans of each other. For service club business I had to communicate between them like a tween caught between divorced parents. The Christmas toy drive was the biggest operation to wrangle, and they bickered as Mrs. Murphy searched through paper stacks on her chaotic desk for the request lists from local charities. Michelle and I focused on the marketing campaign. We hit it hard with promotional posters for every homeroom.

Students brought in so many toy donations, we far exceeded Mrs. Murphy's lists. There was a huge overflow of toys stored in the biology lab, stacks of unwrapped inventory growing every day. The tables used for dissecting frogs and grasshoppers were covered with shiny Lego sets, Connect Four boxes and plastic doctor kits.

"We have to find another place to donate all the extra toys," Mrs. Murphy told me, maneuvering herself through gift piles. Occasionally she took the elevator up to the third floor to see how we were doing with the gift wrapping. You could always hear her approaching with her long lanyard of jingling keys. "We have so much surplus," she said, picking up a baby doll and glancing at it. "Way more than we need for our lists." She flung the doll carelessly back on the heap. Her hands were a museum display of class rings in varying gold bulk. Mrs. Murphy had had an extensive education herself and she was damn proud of it.

Jugenheimer spoke from the doorway, where he'd materialized from his room next door. "Well, you'd better sort it out and get wrapping," he snapped. "We deliver at the end of the week."

"I'm sorting it out!" Mrs. Murphy barked. She looked at me, as if to say, *can you believe this guy?* You had to hand it to her. She didn't take any of his crap. The new Bio teacher, on the other hand, had cried after Jugenheimer yelled at her in the hallway for forgetting to turn her homeroom TV on for morning announcements.

"It doesn't look like it," Jugie said. He executed a power move by keeping his slide-out unhurried.

It seemed like a good problem to have, and an answer presented itself on that night's *Action News*. The Salvation Army in North Philly had a shortage of gifts for kids in need this Christmas and was putting out a call for toy donations.

The next day Michelle and I headed to Guidance and wormed our way past the nun henchwoman to Mrs. Murphy's desk. I updated her on the news report. I said the Salvation Army would be the perfect place to bring all the extras.

"We can't bring them there," Mrs. Murphy said. "They have to go to a Catholic charity."

"What's the difference?" Michelle said. "We have them, and they need them."

"No," Mrs. Murphy said fiercely, chopping the air with both hands. "Father Jugenheimer would lose it. We'll just give extra to the group home."

Michelle and I walked back out to the hallway and looked at each other.

"This is bullshit," Michelle said.

It hadn't been for nothing that I'd gone to those panels on wealth redistribution at last summer's convention protests. It hadn't been for nothing that on Thanksgiving I had listened to the entirety of Arlo Guthrie's eighteen-minute protest song *Alice's Restaurant* on NPR. This was a Robin Hood situation.

I leaned in toward Michelle. "We're gonna steal the extra presents and deliver them ourselves."

Between classes the rest of the day, we worked out a strategy. Like I said, Michelle was someone who got things done. She tapped her friend Mary Kate, who had a Twilight Blue Pearl '89 Dodge Daytona. She explained the heist and that we needed a getaway car and driver. Mary Kate was in.

There were a number of moving pieces. We had to figure out how to get the presents from the third-floor lab on one end of the school to Mary Kate's car on the other side of the building without being noticed.

Michelle was a natural at organizing a covert assembly line because she was a smoker. The girls who smoked had a prison style system to share cigarettes during the school day. The first smoker would leave class and go to the girls' room, go into the designated stall, and take out a Newport that had been stashed in the toilet paper holder. She'd light it, take a puff, and blow the smoke into her baggy navy uniform sweater. (You couldn't blow the smoke up because the Guidance Nun liked to sneak attack the bathrooms for telltale smoke above the stalls.) Then, she'd put out the partly smoked cigarette and either stash it in the toilet paper holder for the next girl or, if she sat near the next smoker in class, wrap it in toilet paper, stick it in her shirt pocket, and deposit it into the girl's schoolbag back in the classroom. Then that girl would ask to go to the bathroom and the cycle would continue. The shorted cigarettes smelled like wet garbage and the sweaters smelled like Irish bookies packed with old men watching televised horse races circa 1972. The teachers didn't notice, or chose not to. The point is, it was a very organized system.

The toy smuggling had to be just as tight. After school, Michelle was to get the car lined up, and I was to man the gift-wrapping station until it was time. Service club members wrapped gifts for an hour, leaving one by one to go home. I waited until just a few senior girls were left and pulled them into a huddle.

"Listen," I whispered, explaining the operation. No one hesitated. We started filling black contractor trash bags with toys as fast as we could. Barbie dolls, soccer balls, Tickle Me Elmo. The key was to take a decent amount, but not so much that it was noticeable. We loaded six bags and lined them up near the doorway.

Michelle entered the room. "Mary Kate's ready when we are," she said. The team regrouped. I reiterated the plan on my palm.

The Runner would take a bag of toys from the lab and ferry it down the long hallway to the Hauler. The Hauler would run the bag down three flights of stairs and hand it to Michelle, who'd be propping the door open. Michelle would load the bag into Mary Kate's open hatchback, parked at the door with Mary Kate in the driver's seat and the engine running in case we needed to make a quick escape. Then the Hauler would run back upstairs and give me a wave to signal she was ready for the next bag. I'd be Lookout, stationed in the middle of the hallway, and would turn back and give the signal to the Runner.

I paced up and down, checking for teachers. Mrs. Murphy was coming up and down on the elevator regularly to check in. I tiptoed by Jugie's room. It was locked and quiet.

I was jumpy but juiced up. This was combining all my favorite things. Telling people what to do. Sneaking around. Sticking it to the man.

The Hauler appeared from the stairwell at the end of the hallway and made a motion with her hand. I immediately realized I shouldn't have been the Lookout. I couldn't tell if she was making a "Good to go" wave or a "Mayday!" gesture. I had just gotten contact lenses that year and had a lot of trouble with them, and even when I got up a half hour early every day to work on sticking them to my eyeballs, two out of five days of the week I ended up going to school with just one contact in. Today was a one-good-eye day.

I covered my fuzzy eye with one hand, squinted and bent my knees. It was a "Good to go" wave. I turned to the Runner at the starting block in the lab doorway. "Go!"

She dragged the first bag of toys down the hall. The Hauler grabbed it and headed down the stairs. In two minutes, she was back, waving for the next one. The Runner delivered two more bags. The elevator was sure to ding soon with Mrs. Murphy. I had no idea where Jugenheimer was. If he caught us, he would probably spontaneously combust while squeaking *"Excommunication!"* Who would teach senior religion? Maybe I could take over. We'd start with Bob Marley and "Get Up Stand Up."

The last load was all hands on deck. The Runner raced down the stairwell and I followed with the final two bags, squinting my good eye. At the bottom of the stairs, the Hauler held the door, the Runner put her bags in the car, and Michelle sat shotgun as I heaved in the last bag and slammed the trunk.

"That's it!" I said. We all waved, and Mary Kate was off, cigarette hanging out of her mouth, gunning out of the school parking lot and headed for Broad Street with tires squealing.

Mrs. Murphy wandered back in at some point to find us wrapping gifts. She didn't notice anything. Mary Kate and Michelle drove down Broad Street until they saw the Salvation Army, right there next to the Divine Lorraine Hotel. They dropped off the toys. The staff were glad to get them.

I was satisfied. I had pulled off a heist with one good eye.

Mrs. Murphy stayed at our high school until it closed permanently; the archdiocesan piggy bank was scraped clean from all the child abuse lawsuits. Jugie took a parish position in Wisconsin where he is properly homesteading and making maple syrup.

Michelle runs her own event planning company now. Oh, and I mastered the contact lens situation in good time. I didn't want you to be worried.

Protecting My Duck's Virginity

I WORKED AT A FARM camp for several summers. We led kids around two hundred sixty acres of wood, meadow, creek, and pond, catching frogs and getting dirty. One year at the start of the camp season, Jenna, who worked at the farm year-round, brought me a duckling. A former camper had found it in the woods behind their house. A fox had gotten the mother, probably.

I had the youngest kids, kindergarten age, and a high schooler assistant. We were given the duckling as our pet for the summer. He was yellow and brown and fluffy, and fit in the palm of my hand. We named him Ping, after the picture book.

We kept Ping in an old glass aquarium tank with a heat lamp. As he got bigger, we moved him to a wider cage and allowed the kids to carefully take him out and hold him. We started taking Ping along when we went to play in the woods or the creek, carrying him in a basket with a cloth over his head like a 19th century baroness keeping the sun off. Eventually Ping outgrew the basket and started walking with us. We tramped all over camp, a row of ten kids and a duck following at the end of the line. It was so adorable, you could have thrown up.

Ping wasn't the only animal at farm camp. The barnyard had pet goats, chickens, sheep, and the cow, T-Bone. T-Bone was a world-weary veteran who had been occupying his field for years like a rent control tenant. To be honest, at his age it was a daily relief to see that he had made it to the morning. You never knew. One night a goat named Roslyn escaped her pen, got into the feed bag in the barn and ate herself to death.

Visiting the goat pen required strategy. My high schooler assistant would serve as bouncer and restrain our kids until I gave the signal. My job was to hold the gate open just wide enough for the kids to get in without the goats getting out. I'd squeeze inside, holding the gate with one hand while yelling "Go! Go! Go!" as the kids scrambled through with panicked faces. The goats would gallop over to escape, and I'd body check them to fend them off. Cesar, the three-hundred-pound leader, liked doing a fake and drive. He'd barrel out of the pen, dragging me from behind with my arms wrapped around his rump in a hopeless embrace. At this point, the campers went wild. "Cesar's out! Cesar's out!" Cesar, running free in aimless circles like a streaker at a World Series game, had to be run down and lured back to the pen with a bucket of feed. The kids cheered.

There were ducks, too, heartless fellows that roomed in the goat pen and ganged up on the one female duck to let nature take its course, pecking the back of her head as they did so. It got to the point the female had to seek asylum in an undisclosed location on the other side of camp.

We'd assumed Ping was a male duck, which meant he would join the others in the goat pen when he got big enough by the end of summer. Midway through the camp season, new feathers came in and he transformed into a mottled brown and white. He didn't have the brightly colored feather that male mallards have. Jenna inspected and confirmed it. He was a she.

Everyone adjusted their pronouns. We had a new problem: where would Ping go at the end of camp?

Jenna explained the duck mating process to me. As we'd seen, male ducks could get violent in taking the female. The duck penis is, horrifyingly, shaped like a spiky corkscrew. This makes the whole thing even more brutal, and females evolve to protect themselves against giving birth to the offspring of overly aggressive males. The female duck vagina is not a single canal, but a house of mirrors situation, full of false passageways and clockwise stairs to nowhere. If a female duck doesn't want to have a male duck's babies, she can send his sperm through her corn maze of an organ into a cul-de-sac dead end. Sort of like going to IKEA; you're trying to get meatballs but end up in a 240-square-foot simulated apartment with artificial succulents.

Jenna elaborated that if the duck decides she does want to have a particular mate's offspring, she is able to relax her muscles and allow her guest to follow the blinking light to the right destination.

I was impressed. What if the human female reproductive system could do such tricks? There'd be a whole troupe of ushers in there, with name tags and lanyards: "Right this way sir, you wanna go this way," waving in one direction and then whispering to the side, "Close the northwest tunnel, we do not wanna have this guy's baby ... He is mean to his mother and he's a Patriots fan."

Knowing what we knew, I did not want Ping to be put in with the randy male ducks in the goat pen. I was ready to put her in a 1910s bathing suit, cover her ankles, and stand threateningly in front of the males with a shotgun like the dad in *Footloose*.

Jenna assured me it wouldn't be a problem. We could put Ping on the other side of the barn near the chicken coop when it was time.

Ping was the star of the summer. The he-to-she adventure lent her even more glamor. Our kids may have been the littlest in camp, but Ping was theirs. They marched across pastures with pride. Ping hurried to catch up and was the mascot for all activities, pecking on the sidelines without judgment. As she grew, other groups asked special permission to borrow her for sessions at the creek. She was the most popular animal at the farm.

I felt the gravity of caretaking a duck treasured by all. When she outgrew her cage, it would be on my shoulders to make sure she was all right. I resolved to make sure none of the males laid a feather on her.

On the last day of camp, I took Ping to the new home I'd prepared, far away from the other ducks, inside the barn where she could roost. During the day when the barn door was unlocked, she could join the chickens in free ranging. In witness protection with the hens, she'd remain untouched.

It was a strange feeling to see her settled into her hay. I had raised Ping from a baby, and now she was on her own in the big world. "Goodbye," I said. She looked back, indifferent. I remembered how eager I'd been for my parents to leave when they dropped me off at college. I turned and walked away.

The next spring, I got a text from Jenna. I immediately got into my car, drove the hour to the farm and walked over to the chicken coop. There were four fluffy black-and-yellow ducklings, and Ping, now fully grown with a wide belly and ridged red face mask, stood behind them.

Someone had knocked up my duck.

How had this happened? I started to get angry at the cads who must have busted through their pen, but then remembered the magic vagina. If a female duck didn't want to be inseminated, she could stop it from happening. The deal only gets sealed when she chooses the mate. That meant … Ping hadn't been assaulted. She was in love.

I looked across the chicken coop. You might not think it's possible for a duck to look smug, but Ping radiated the essence of a woman expecting a diamond necklace for a push present.

Jenna explained. Ping liked to step out and free range during the day. Unlike the domesticated species of males who had their wings clipped, Ping was a mallard duck born wild and could fly. So she would roam all over the farm and swoop in and out of the animal pens. She must have taken a liking to one of the male ducks she saw on her visits.

I wished we knew the details. Were there long walks around the corral full of *Son of a Preacher Man* sweet talk? Had she done the seducing herself? Did it happen in the moonlight, at least?

Jenna said they had no idea Ping had laid eggs; she hid the nest up in the hayloft until they hatched that morning. The whole thing was kept secret, like the Irish Magdalene Laundries where they sent pregnant girls into hiding for nine months.

When you thought about it, it was just like her to have a secret affair and surprise everyone. After all I had done to protect her innocence, Ping had liberated herself. She was her own woman from start to finish. "I support your choices," I said softly through the chicken wire. "I'm proud of you."

I tried to catch her eye, to dispel any resentment; see if she knew me. She played it cool.

Marie Kondo Was Not a Football Fan

IN 1992 MY BROTHER STARTED working as a paperboy. It was in time for the Eagles playoffs and the following year's Phillies World Series run. He always had leftover newspapers, which meant there were extra *Daily News* sports pages for me to cut up and put on my bedroom wall. I taped pictures of quarterback Randall Cunningham and running back Herschel Walker to the wood paneling, next to my thin fleecy Eagles pennant. In '93, I added Phillies lefties John Kruk and Darren Daulton. Not long after, I stood in line on a hot July afternoon in a neighborhood beer distributor parking lot to get an autograph from centerfield icon and radio sportscaster Richie Ashburn.

In 2001 I kept clippings from Allen Iverson's Sixers championship series against the Lakers. I saved the glossy *Inquirer* keepsake poster from the '05 Eagles Super Bowl heartbreaker against the Patriots. In '08, I was at Citizens Bank Park with a standing room ticket the night the Phillies won the Series. I handed my rally towel to one of the groundskeepers to rub in the baseline dirt.

If none of this means anything to you, that's okay. The point is, when you grow up in Philly, at least one area of your house serves as a museum celebrating hometown teams. You have to start curating your collection as a child. If you do a respectable job, you should have a decent start by the time you move out of your parents' house.

A friend told me about Marie Kondo's decluttering book when it came out, and I read it in one sitting. It was a small book with a cloudy blue hardback cover. Marie was earnest about keeping only the things you love. She said you should thank each item before getting rid of it, and she promised you wouldn't regret throwing anything away. I dumped letters I had saved for decades, papers written in college, photos from high school dances, and pounds of t-shirts. I brought carloads of donations to the thrift store.

I kept my sports memorabilia.

Not long after I had Kondoed, I started talking to a guy on a dating app who happened to work on the coaching staff of the Philadelphia Eagles.

Yes. I know.

It was the era of head coach Chip Kelly. The city had a love/hate relationship with Chip. The guy was either trash or a Christ figure. (Christ figure isn't safer; after worship comes being offered up for sacrifice.) In case you weren't clear on this, home team devotion in Philly leans violent. During the '93 Series, closing pitcher Mitch Williams got death threats from his own fans.

With Chip in his third season and the city on edge with overdue hopes for a Super Bowl, I had a direct line to one of his guys, someone on the inside.

For a week, I exchanged messages with my coach over the app. I was aware I had to exercise ultimate restraint. I made it clear I was a football fan, but I knew there was a delicate line between acknowledging his work and acting no more impressed than if he repaired HVAC. I couldn't have him think the Eagles thing was the only reason I was talking to him. (Was it? *Do not think too much about this.*) When I walked into the bar to meet my coach in person for the first time, I yelled at myself in my head: *PLAY. IT. COOL.*

The date was fun. We chatted during the following week and went on to see each other regularly over the course of the season. It wasn't anything serious. But for me, it carried the mental burden of a full-time job.

I already watched weekly games and read the sports page write-ups after, but now I felt on assignment to get in the weeds with the injury reports for the entire NFL, just to make sure he knew that I knew my stuff if it came up. I stalked the team's Twitter feed on a regular basis and screen-grabbed photos of my coach at practice in case anybody asked for proof. I studied a Rand McNally of the continental U.S. to decide how far I'd be willing to move if he got recruited to be a head coach in the Midwest. (Minnesota: no. Green Bay: maybe?)

The thing is … the team was not doing well. Was it my fault? Was my coach doing a poor job breaking tape because we stayed up too late the other night, causing a foggily judged play call and Miami's interception in the fourth quarter? Dunkin' Donuts gave out free coffee on Mondays when the Eagles won. How could I bear being the one responsible for everyone grumping into work with a cracked thermos of instant instead of getting in the victory line? The weight of the city's happiness was on my shoulders. My face was sure to be in the news when sports reporters pinpointed me as the root of the team's failure. They'd probably call me "unknown woman," and that would be the worst part of all.

One Sunday I was at my parents' house to watch the game. The cameras zoomed in on the coaches' box, and there he was, yelling through his headset. I was thrilled but terrified. If my extended family found out I was hanging out with someone within the organization, they'd demand I bring him to Christmas, then grill him on what the hell was going on with the offensive strategy and insist he deliver their suggestions and threatening messages to Chip Kelly. I envisioned him accosted over the bowl of homemade cannoli filling, unable to finish loading up his shell because everyone was on his ass. It would be embarrassing.

Another thing was bothering me. There was something on my bookshelf that I didn't want my coach to notice.

A year earlier I had worked a catering shift at an event for the Philadelphia Eagles owners and higher-ups. VIP events weren't unusual for our company. I had done a Sixers Foundation event attended by Dr. Oz. (He ambled by my buffet spread of pork fried dumplings and cheesesteak egg rolls, shooting the messenger with a judgy smile.) I'd worked a bar mitzvah for a kid with his own sneaker company, and I once presented a plate of bleeding steak to the mayor's wife, who looked at me coolly and said, "I don't eat red meat."

Our manager had warned us at orientation that we'd be fired on the spot if we ever behaved inappropriately around famous guests. No ogling, no acting weird, no talking besides "You're welcome" or answering a question. If it would even cross your mind to ask for a selfie, leave now.

There hadn't been any events where the warning would be relevant to me, until that one. A few Eagles players were doing photo ops in front of the team-logo step and repeat: center Jason Kelce, cornerback Brandon Boykin, and tight end Brent Celek.

I was on appetizers. Waiting for the chef to put platters under the countertop warmer, I circled the room casually, pretending to collect empty glasses but in reality homing in on my target. I was aware of the players' every move the same way you would track a high school crush from cafeteria to biology lab, and I had a strategy.

If you were serving appetizers that came on a little stick, you were supposed to have someone follow you to collect the sticks immediately after people finished their two bites.

But I was going solo, baby. I didn't want anyone getting in my way. When the appetizers came out of the kitchen, I grabbed my platter of tooth-pick-spiked, goat cheese-stuffed dates and bolted straight for Kelce, Boykin, and Celek.

The guys smiled gratefully and plucked three dates per hand. I took a step back. Timing was everything. As they bit fruit from toothpicks and swallowed, I swooped back in with the empty platter: "I can take those."

It was worth the risk of the cardinal sin. I got a handful of appetizer sticks and—jackpot—Brent Celek's dirty napkin.

I had my memorabilia. I stuffed everything into my apron pocket.

In catering, the apron pocket is a black hole. Trash, the menu specifying all ingredients and allergens, a Parker House roll painted with butter that you salvaged and planned to swallow without chewing when you got a chance to duck behind a stone pillar. Things get dirty in the apron pocket. Things get lost. I couldn't take any chances.

I went to the bar and leaned over the shiny granite. "Do you have any baggies?" Our bartender handed me a box of clear plastic food gloves. I put the napkin and appetizer sticks into a glove and tied it closed as he watched.

"What are you doing?" he asked.

"I got Brent Celek's napkin," I said, excited.

A server next to me overheard and warned, "Do not post a photo of that."

What kind of person did she think I was? I put the glove bag into my pocket and for the rest of the night was aware of its presence as if it were a living creature. When I got home, I emptied the pocket. I found a plastic sandwich bag that was sturdier than the food glove. I put the appetizer sticks and the napkin into the bag and sealed it, and I put the bag on my bookshelf in a little cardboard tray.

You know what happened next. I read Marie Kondo and turned into Ralph Waldo Emerson, but I kept all my sports mementos. Including the napkin bag.

The first time my Eagles coach saw my place, he said, "What are you, a minimalist?" I explained about Marie Kondo.

"I only kept things that are deeply meaningful to me," I said. As I said it, my eyes passed over my bookshelf, where the napkin bag sat in the cardboard tray.

Shit.

If he saw the napkin bag and I admitted what it was, he would think I had some kind of fanatic thing towards sports players and I was only hanging out with him because of his proximity. (Was I? *Do not think too much about this.*)

I could hide the bag in the medicine cabinet. Or in a drawer, or under the bed. But people look in medicine cabinets. Or he might go in the drawer or find himself under the bed. What if I emerged one day from the bathroom to find my coach holding up the baggie in victory, shouting "Oh ho ho! What's THIS?!" What is my explanation for hoarding trash? It would be weirder to keep it under the bed than on the shelf, right?

The team wasn't looking good at 6 wins and 8 losses, and the napkin bag was ripe for discovery.

On December 26th, the Eagles lost to Washington. No playoffs. After the game, I went to my coach's house to commiserate over a drink. Wandering around the apartment, I noticed an unopened Christmas present on the floor next to his bed with a computer-printed label reading FROM: CHIP in Garamond font. In the open closet was a stack of fresh, tagged team apparel.

Marie Kondo talked about how it was essential to get rid of things from your past to make room for the new. If I couldn't let go of the old, my hands wouldn't be open to receive a signed jersey or (hang in there) a championship ring.

I went home. I thanked the napkin bag for the joy it had given me and threw it out.

Three days later Chip Kelly was fired.

The dominoes fell down the line. My coach got the ax. He left the state, and I never saw him again. The napkin bag was gone forever.

I regret it.

I Fixed My Car Myself

I HAD JUST SPLIT FROM a boyfriend and was eating heartbreak daily. I walked through woods for hours like Cheryl Strayed in *Wild* and did Sudoku in bed at night (the kind for beginners). It was July. One day I drove to the South Jersey beach town where my parents were vacationing. My mom and I waded in the water by the lifeguard stand and talked about everyday things while the sea wind blasted around us.

It was a good beach day. I got sand all over the front seat and drove over the Ocean City bridge headed for home.

The oil light on my Honda had been on for a few days, and I'd been pushing off dealing with it. I was worried about the long drive home. I found it exciting to play Russian roulette with the gas tank ("Kramer and the car salesman drove with the slash below E for miles on that one *Seinfeld* episode; I can go another twenty minutes") but I'd learned that neglecting the oil too long can lead to expensive consequences. My friend Pete had once shown me how to check the oil and how to add some to tide things over before bringing the car in for a change.

I decided I would add oil.

I pulled into a gas station just past the island bridge. It was minimalist: two gas pumps and a store the size of a gym shower stall. An auto repair shop was attached. The garage door was open, and a mechanic was in the shop working on a car.

I parked to the side of the store so I would have room to do my dirty work and went inside. There were a couple shelves' worth of Mobil oil and some small red and white bags of Herr's ridged potato chips. A gas attendant in a blue uniform came in from the pumps and stood behind the counter, watching me. I looked at the plastic containers of oil and tried to remember things I'd been told. Conventional or synthetic. 10W-30 or 5W20. I was taking too long. This guy would think I didn't know what I was doing.

How many should I get? The oil light had been on for a significant amount of time; the car had to be thirsty. It's always better to make two trays of Rice Krispie treats for a party instead of one. It's better to bring three books for a train trip than just one. (Nonfiction, fiction, and self-help are specific *moods*; how will I know what mood I'll be in?) More is always better.

I put three quart-sized containers of Mobil conventional oil on the counter. The attendant looked like he wanted to say something. He didn't. I paid, carried the oil outside and put it on the ground next to the car.

I popped the hood (I knew how; Pete had shown me), lifted it up (feel with your fingers for the latch and heave; it's heavy, so it feels like you're really doing something) and propped it with the lever (you've rounded first: the hood is now up and you can stand there with hands on hips like an expert). The gas attendant came out of the store and stood there, watching.

I said, "Is it okay I'm doing this here?" He motioned as if to say, *you need help?* I waved him off. "No, I got it!" I said. He nodded, smiled, and went over to sit on the cement block next to the gas pumps. I don't think he had much English. He kept watching me. *You want a performance, buddy? I'll give you a performance.*

The oil cap was easy; it was labeled. I unscrewed it and put it on the ground. The orange ring was the dipstick. I loved the dipstick because it had a fun name. A classic insult, dipstick. Plus the under-utilized shortened version, "dip."

I knew there was some sort of dress rehearsal with the dipstick where you took it out, wiped it off, put it back in and took it out again. I grabbed the orange ring and pulled the dipstick out. It was a long, floppy metal stick, and seemed too flimsy to have any real responsibility. I stuck it back in the holder and pulled it out again.

I stared at the little hatch marks and dots on the stick. There was a suggestion of pale brown; it could have been a trick of the light. I couldn't remember what I was supposed to be looking at. I looked up. The attendant was still sitting there, watching. I put the dipstick in one more time, pulled it out, and stared at it again. Then I nodded to myself (*accurate reading, boss; send the numbers to headquarters*) and stuck it back in.

What was the difference? The car needed oil. I would add oil.

I picked up the first quart container. I would add all the oil I had; if it started to overflow, I would stop. Not complicated.

I opened the first quart and started pouring. It made a satisfying *glug glug* sound. The mechanic from the shop poked his head out. He was wiping his hands on a rag, and he surveyed me for a second, then went back into the garage. The attendant addressed a customer and pumped their gas, then returned to his cement block to watch me. He might as well have had popcorn.

I started the second quart. *Glug glug glug.* The mechanic stuck his head out again, went back in. I felt smug. Just a woman alone in an Eagles hat over wet pigtails, cropped sweatpants and tank top, sand still everywhere. Confidently taking care of her car. My hands were black with grease. *I am such a badass.*

This was whetting my appetite to make a habit of working on the car myself. Why go somewhere to get it fixed when I could do things on my own? I could take some classes and get trained up in changing my own oil and replacing parts. I'd be out on my block under the hood, and everybody would say, *There she is, she fixes her own car.* I could make YouTube videos about DIY auto repairs and get a necklace with a crescent wrench pendant. *She's such a Renaissance woman!* I'd wear strictly jumpsuits from now on, the long-sleeve canvas ones with a tie belt. I love jumpsuits, so this was good.

I poured in the third quart of oil. *Glug glug glug.* I put the oil cap on, let the hood slam, and put the plastic oil containers in the trash can. I got in the car and turned the key.

A black cloud of smoke erupted from the hood.

The attendant, watching from his cement block, stood up.

The smoke cloud grew bigger, and blacker, and billowed around the sides of the car. Okay. Maybe it would stop in a second. Maybe the car was just having an adjustment period.

The mechanic looked out.

Pretend nothing is happening. Drive. I pulled around slowly from the side of the store. The smoke kept coming, thick. It was not nothing.

Options. Refuse to make eye contact with anyone; keep driving; possibly die. Stop, get out and open hood in front of both attendant and mechanic. Stop, stay in car and do nothing.

I eased forward a few more feet. Now I was directly in front of the garage. I couldn't see ahead of me through the smoke still pouring from the hood. *This is a thing.*

The mechanic ran over, rag in hand. "What'd you do?!" he yelled.

I couldn't ignore him. I turned off the car, opened the door and front-crawled through the smoke cloud.

"What'd you do?!" he said again. He was friendly, not pissed off. We both stood at a distance from the car, waving our hands against the fumes.

"I don't know," I said. "I put in oil."

He shook his head, like he couldn't believe it. "I thought you knew what you were doing!"

He asked how much oil I had put in and reacted when I told him three quarts.

"Oh no! You gotta get that extra oil out," he said. "I'll put it up on the lift and we'll drain it out."

The mechanic got in my car and backed it into the garage; exhaust filled the shop and then floated slowly out and over the lot like a mushroom cloud. The attendant was still standing near his cement block, watching, silent. I wished he would make any kind of expression or motion, just to indicate that he was a participant in this.

The mechanic waved me in. He told me to stand to the side while he got the car on the lift and elevated it toward the ceiling. We introduced ourselves. His name was José. He said he would drain the oil out, change it and get things sorted.

Then he said, "I was watching you, like, I guess she knows what she's doing! Don't you got a husband or boyfriend who can help you with this stuff?"

The line would have been edited out of a screenplay. It was too obvious. My boyfriend of a year and a half HAD been good with cars. He'd easily changed a flat on the side of the road. He replaced my brake light using his own tools. (To be fair, I did a beautiful job organizing his spice drawer with magnetic circular jars from The Container Store. We broke up two weeks later.)

In the movie version, I'd burst into tears and tell José everything. Instead, I said, "No, I don't! That's why I'm trying to do it myself!"

José laughed. "I'll show you," he said. "You're not supposed to be in here, but just stand over there and you can watch and I'll explain what I'm doing."

I looked at my Honda up on the lift. I had never seen it from this angle. José set an oil pan on the ground and unscrewed the drain plug under the car. A stream of oil gushed out and splattered into the pan; it kept coming and coming, a never-ending, resentful chute of brown. I'd overserved a sorority girl, and now she had to get her stomach pumped. "I'm sorry," I whispered.

José went in and out of the open garage door, dealing with other customers. I stayed at my post. There was so much to see: barrels of fluid, toolboxes, trays with a dozen containers for different screws and bolts and washers. I wished I had my notebook; I would write everything down. I started to get excited. Hadn't I just been thinking I wanted to learn? This time I would pay attention, really listen.

Years ago, I had a summer when I was in multiple weddings. Instead of paying to get my makeup done I decided I would go to a department store makeup counter, get a real tutorial, and buy the right stuff once and for all. I was living in New York, and I went to Bloomingdales on Fifth Avenue, where everything is shiny. I went to the Bobbi Brown counter and explained my situation to a girl with extreme eyebrows. She was delighted. She showed me how undereye concealer should be dabbed on using only the ring finger and how to use different eyeshadow colors in succession from brow bone to eye crease. Why couldn't car tutorials stick with me the way the makeup lesson did?

This was why I mechanic hopped. I was afraid to build a relationship with a mechanic, because I knew I would automatically trust them for no good reason. When I don't understand what's going on, I put too much stock in the people who know better. "Here's my hair. Just put some layers in? Or whatever you think? I trust you."

I act like I understand, but we both know I don't really know what I'm talking about. We're both aware that at the end of the exchange, they will say "Give me your money" and I will say "Here it is, no questions asked."

Never again. The jumpsuit fantasy merged with a movie version. José would be my tutor. I'd confess my heartbreak; he'd speak in car metaphors as he taught me the basics. My face would read rebirth and then determination. *Montage to The Pussycat Dolls' I Don't Need a Man: Me studying under the hood with José, handing him the tools. Me taking some night classes in auto repair. Me coming back, showing José how my car is doing: "The alternator needed tuning, so I got under there and gave it a three-quarter crank and she was good to go." Then a role reversal: José handing me the tools as I crack a tough job on a Jeep. We high five. On the way home, I pull to the side of the road to help some guy in khakis who's stranded. I show him how to check his oil; he gives me his number.*

Somebody started yelling at the garage entrance. I looked over. A guy with white hair, a Knicks jersey and a gold chain was pedaling in on a fat-tire bike.

"Oh no. Here we go," José said.

"What's goin' on?" the guy yelled. "Who's this?"

He hopped off his bike, parked it and introduced himself as Tommy: the owner of the shop and another one up the highway. He lived down the street.

"I put too much oil in," I said.

Tommy said, "You by yourself? Where's your boyfriend? He should be doin' this."

Seriously. It was terrible writing. I wasn't even mad.

"I don't have one," I said. *Know your audience; do not deliver feminist treatise.* "That's why I'm learning. José's showing me."

"You need a friend? Come over, I'll be your friend. You wanna come over for dinner? My mother's making meatballs. White house, down the street. Ring the bell."

Tommy got back on his bike and pedaled off, saying, "I'll be back."

For the next hour Tommy popped in and out while José worked between my car and another vehicle. He explained everything about the oil:

why it mattered how much was in there; how to read the dipstick. He told me about coolant and how I needed to check that too. "You gotta learn," he said.

I was so excited. Things would be different from now on. I was going to be a woman who knew how to take care of her car. I'd even wash it myself. With a bucket of soapy water and a thick sponge.

The job was finished, and I paid at the counter. There were Bible quotes taped to the wall by the register. I thanked José over and over. I said I would stop by next time I was going to Ocean City. He gave me his card.

The attendant watched me start my car and pull out. He was still silent.

I rolled down my windows to get the breeze and waited at the lot exit to break into the line of traffic. Tommy rolled by on his bike and spoke through the window. "Come over. I'll be your friend. I'm serious."

"Thanks," I said. I drove away.

The next time my car needed servicing, I immediately gave up the fantasy and took it to Pep Boys. It's been two years. I told myself I would go back sometime, bring José a couple Gatorades, but I never did.

How to Give Someone Your Number

IT WAS WEDDING SEASON IN my twenties.

This sets the scene (i.e., "It was a dark and stormy night;" "It was a Tuesday on the Wal Mart loading dock") and introduces the concept (i.e., "During my twenties, everyone around me was getting married"). It was wedding season, and it was *wedding season*.

We can all recite the checklist of what it entails. We know the equation: number of weddings (x) is inverse to the amount of disposable funds available (y) during the given life era ($a1$). After crying over the numbers, you get yourself a weekend job. You have to pretend that you can afford the lineup of events so as not to upset the bride. After all, they're pretending they can afford to hold said festivities. If anyone knocks a card out of place, the whole house will fall, and then what will happen to the calligraphy industry? Where will the harpists find work?

It was during wedding season that I attended a different celebration: my friend Chantal's mom, Simone, was graduating from a doctoral program and I joined the family and friends for the ceremony and celebration. It was refreshing. The featured speaker was not talking about happy couples. I'd just attended a church wedding where the priest, in between offering a prayer for the souls of the dead and for those living with cancer, prayed for the single people "who have not yet found love."

I didn't have to wear a bachelorette tank top that said "Sexy 3" that matched Sexy 2, Sexy 4, Sexy 5, Sexy 6, and Sexy 7 (the bride was Sexy 1). I didn't have to attend a bridal party and keep track of the gifts (*from Rebecca: stainless steel apple divider and meat thermometer*) while someone next to me stuck gift bows onto a paper plate to make a hat for the overwhelmed bride who was opening boxes of thongs in front of her great-aunts. All I had to do was put on my Payless gold slingback heels and go to an Italian restaurant.

We went to La Viola, a little BYO in Philadelphia's Rittenhouse Square. The wait staff pushed together a bunch of four-tops and Chantal, her parents, and the rest of the cast of characters squeezed in around the long banquet setting in front of the window looking over Sixteenth Street. Simone had a group of friends of all different ages and backgrounds. No matter who I talked to, I always ended up hearing someone's fascinating life story and grabbing a pen to write down their profound words.

I ate bread with olive oil and red pepper flakes and talked with Sandra, a vintage clothing boutique owner seated next to me, about the last guy I dated. She said some people are weeds in our garden and some are flowers. I nodded and reached for my notebook. Connor, a grad student with a ponytail, told a story about bringing a girl back to his place, where he had no bed. He slept on a wooden floor, because "Why do I have to be comfortable while I'm unconscious?" We made fun of him and laughed and called down the table to each other. I felt better about being recently disentangled from someone, having no "and guest" to bring to the summer's upcoming wedding lineup. Life felt wide open.

When Connor stood up to take a cigarette break, I noticed a busboy at the back of the room bringing dirty glasses into the kitchen. I couldn't see him that well. It was more an outline, an impression. But from where I sat, he looked cute. I had an idea.

The wait staff put our plates in front of us. (I'd automatically ordered the penne, the bargain-basement item of Italian restaurants.) When Connor returned to his seat, I whispered to him and Sandra.

"That busboy back there is cute. Should I leave him my number?"

Joey, who wore a leather jacket and ran a cupcake shop, whipped around. "Yes!" he said with excitement. Sandra nodded. Connor looked to the back, squinted, and frowned. "That meathead?"

"I'm going to do it," I said. "After dinner!"

We all whispered and giggled, but we still didn't have a great view. He only crossed the floor once, and there were people blocking him. But he had dark hair; he had to be Italian, and I'm Italian, so, you know. He was probably the owner's son, putting in hours while he finished his MBA to eventually take over the restaurant. We could get together and eventually run the place as a family, and I could offer classes in pasta-making in the basement. (I could learn.)

What a perfect how-we-met story this was going to be. Finally, something exciting to write about in my journal. (Last week's entry: *Saturday night, 9:20 pm. Went to see* Wall-E *alone. Came home, shook popcorn out of bra.*) This was a bold new beginning, and you know when you *know*? I just knew. Not only would he be my "and guest" for this summer's events, he would be more than that. After all those cattle calls to the dance floor to catch a bouquet, my turn was here.

Boy, was I going to stick it to everyone. My mind worked fast. In between our server removing the dinner plates and Simone ordering a round of cappuccinos, I had the whole lineup of wedding events sketched out for me and my busboy.

THE ANNOUNCEMENT

This is where I would get back at all the people who sent a group text about their engagement after not hearing from them in years. I get it. You have to scrape together some warm bodies to fill the brunch bench for the proposal story. Can we stop pretending it's not about an audience, though? Can we just lean in? For my engagement announcement, I would rent a high school auditorium, take the mic and walk everyone through a slideshow, TEDx style. If the event was about me telling the story, then let me do it up, beginning with my birth and childhood.

THE ENGAGEMENT PHOTOS

Right here in the restaurant, Lady-and-the-Tramping one piece of spaghetti, red sauce all over our white outfits like a vat of ravioli was just murdered. Instead of sharing them on social media I would print them out on glossy 8x10s and stick one through the mailbox every week up until the wedding. Just so they wouldn't forget.

THE SAVE THE DATE

Singing telegrams. They would all get singing telegrams. No need to cover the poison control number on the fridge with a photo of la fiancée's heavy left hand. A man in a crushed velvet suit would be at their door to sing "Funiculi Funicula," pass over a handwritten index card and throw a handful of confetti into the house.

THE BRIDAL SHOWER

Back-to-back screenings of *Godfather I* and *II*. Once you were in, you weren't leaving. All doors would be locked.

THE INVITATION

I needed Working Hands lotion for my chapped fingers after opening thick invitations all year, handling envelopes inside envelopes, extraneous tissue

paper, printed-out driving directions, and monogram-printed cardstock. I
would one-up all of it. Everyone was going to get a copy of *Ulysses* (730 pages)
and *Infinite Jest* (1,079 pages). Plus my 40-page research thesis from graduate
school. *Observing Children Documentation, page 14: Jasper picks up a pencil.
He sniffs it. He puts it down. He picks it up again. He sniffs it (cont'd next page).*
Also a ream of printer paper from Staples (free with rebate).

THE BACHELORETTE

Everyone would chip in for a limo that would drive in circles for two hours.
I'd hire an actor friend to throw a fit and cry, and everyone would have to
deal with her all night. I'd be on the other side of the divider in the front seat
sharing a box of Junior Mints with the driver.

THE RECEPTION

Here's where we would bring it all back. The whole wedding would be Italian
restaurant themed. Red checkered plastic tablecloths from the dollar store.
Tubs of lemon and cherry water ice for dessert (separate, not mixed – come
on) (*note to self: remind staff about temperature control.*) I'd hire a local political candidate to do some speeches. Just to offend people, we'd do the Dollar
Dance and circulate a monogrammed velvet bag to collect cash. For the
sendoff, everyone would get a bag of breadcrumbs to toss; instead of doves,
pigeons would swarm.

THE FAVORS

Each guest would get a subscription box with a different photo product of
the couple arriving each month. By the end of the year their houses would
be filled with the faces of me and my busboy eyeing them from phone cases,
coffee mugs, toothbrush holders and toilet paper.

MORE MAIL

I remembered the card from friends that said *The Lovebirds Have Found
Their Nest* with a photo of them in front of their freshly constructed house.

I'd do better than that with a postcard closeup of a bedbug in our one-bed-room apartment.

Joey poked me out of my daydream. The check had arrived. "Write your number on the receipt, and I'll deliver it," he said. The others asked what we were doing. Joey sent word down the table, and the whole group cheered me on. The busboy, still far enough away to be only a silhouette, was in the kitchen doorway. I wrote my name, number, and "Call me!" on the receipt. I was twenty-six years old and I had never left my number for someone like this. I couldn't help smiling.

Joey brought the receipt over to the girl at the host stand. He pointed at me. He pointed to the back. A smile spread over the girl's face, and Joey bounded back to us. We watched as the rest of the wait staff buzzed around the host stand and conferred with the girl like middle schoolers negotiating the terms of pairing friends to slow dance to Celine Dion's *It's All Coming Back to Me Now*.

"Here he comes! They're giving it to him!" Sandra said. I allowed myself one quick glance, but the busboy was surrounded by the others, who were grinning and poking him. They were smiling! They were on my side! "He's walking away," Joey reported. "I'll go see what's up." Connor shook his head and slugged the last of his wine.

Joey came back from the host stand. "They said he's going to meet you out front," he told me.

We all pushed back our wooden chairs to get up. I took a breath and straightened my back. I knew I wasn't going to actually send any singing telegrams, but here was a guy that could be my "and guest." Maybe more. No matter what shape it took, I knew this was going to be something. My stomach fluttered. When you took a risk, you got a reward. This was it.

Everybody moved back to let me go first. I walked out the front door into the early-evening light, and there was the busboy, waiting for me on the front steps in his black and white uniform with my number in his hand. Finally, after everything, I got a good look, an actual look, at his face.

Oh no. Oh no oh no oh no.

It was like being on an airplane. There was nowhere to go. I had to say something. So I said, "Hi. I'm Martha."

"I'm Tim," he said.

He paused.

He said, "I'm fifteen."

…Well.

Have I ever gone back to La Viola? Are you serious?

The Real Nanny of Philadelphia

I WENT TO INTERVIEW FOR a nanny job for seven-month-old Jackson with parents Rachel (doctor) and Keith (MBA student). Rachel asked if I would mind if they had a nanny cam in the house.

"Of course not," I said. "That's great. Everyone should have one." You can't say you mind, because, you know, why would you mind?

I'll tell you why I would mind. It's a violation of the nanny code. When you're out the door, the house is mine, and I eat all your snacks. In a way you won't notice.

The whole joy of nannying is that I'm left alone. No one is judging the way that I wash a bottle or spoon-feed rice cereal. I don't have to explain and justify every move I make with the kid. I take care of business, and at nap time get a couple hours in on whatever creative project I'm working on.

But I needed the job. I took it.

On my first day, I walked up three flights to the apartment and Rachel ran through all the systems and equipment. Have you ever messed with babies? There's a lot going on. Breast milk defrosting, testing the bath temperature, unscrewing the mini brush out of the bottle scrubber to poke through the rubber nipple before sanitizing, restock the diaper bag, nickel-sized dollop of diaper cream, fold the crib sheet like this, teething biscuits that call to mind a British tea service, notebook to track poops, and the spoons go here. "I like everything kept really clean," Rachel said.

Not mentioned: the nanny cam or its location.

If I asked, that would indicate I was concerned about it. If I was concerned about it, that meant I was likely plotting some illicit activity. If I hunted around, that would be caught on camera and rouse suspicion.

It could be anywhere. Were they trying to make it seem less intrusive by not having it out in the open? I had done some Google research. You can buy spy cameras disguised as books, plants, photo frames, light bulbs. The lifeless computer desktop could be recording. Their apartment had so much *stuff*. Wall art, pillows, shelves of knickknacks. Things that looked like smoke alarms and thermostats. But how should I know?

Rachel went to work. It was just me, Jackson, and the camera.

It was a terrible feeling, being watched. I had to be on my best behavior. Every move I made I could feel my brain forming a justification in case I was criticized. "Your honor, the defendant is charged with leaving dirty dishes on the counter." *Objection! If you review it on the tape, my client was momentarily taken away from the task to soothe the crying baby, which you'll agree is the first priority.* "Sustained." "Your honor, the defendant is charged with checking her phone every time it dings, instead of keeping focus on the child." *Objection! My client's duty is to the child's parents as well, and should they message her with requests for updates or photos she must be available with a timely response!* "Sustained. Fitzpatrick, are you going to continue wasting everyone's time? I've got a golf game at four."

I took Jackson out for a walk. The feeling of being observed remained as I got the stroller onto the sidewalk. There was no chance of a camera outside the house ... right? What if it was in the squeaky giraffe in the diaper bag? Could there be a system of hired spies surveilling from front windows?

We came back in. I figured I better narrate to fill in the gaps. "That was so much fun working on your gross motor skills at the play space," I said loudly. "Time to change your diaper! It's important to do it in frequent intervals!"

I dumped a load of Jackson's sleep suits and burp cloths into the laundry. "Let's count to three before we push the start button," I said, balancing him on my hip. "We're practicing numeracy! Your brain synapses are just firing away right now!" That Early Childhood Education master's degree loan of twenty thousand dollars was really paying for itself. (Did I mention it was at an interest rate of 6.8 percent?)

My first day ended. I kept up the perfect nanny drill the next day, and the next. Weeks passed and I started to relax into the routine. Rachel and Keith were happy, and our communication was smooth (still no mention of the camera). I was a *good nanny*. I kept narrating aloud during the day and started to say funny things and be goofy when I felt like it. Really, I should be proud to have this performance on closed-circuit tv.

Maybe … it wasn't so bad being watched.

I now made sure my jokes were loud enough for the cameras. I improvised scenes with Jackson's rubber ducks. I made up songs that were sweet for the baby and full of references for the adults.

This was the Pixar method, wasn't it? Quality material for the kids, and equal attention paid to entertaining the grownups. Maybe I had found my niche.

After all, I had always wanted my own show. Wasn't this … an opportunity, really? It had the potential for hours of material.

Maybe Keith was at a study session with his grad school classmates, checking in on the nanny cam and chuckling. And then his study group would say, "Oh, is that nanny on?" And they'd all gather around to watch: "Oh, she's great. She's so funny." "She's cute, is she single?"

Maybe Rachel and Keith rewatched the tapes at night and laughed. Maybe they forwarded clips to friends. Or there were viewing parties where they got everybody together on Saturday night and featured the week's highlights. What if one of their friends knew somebody who worked in television and realized this was an opportunity for a great new reality show? It might already be live streaming without me knowing it.

Could I ask them to ... see the videos? I could play it all back like Scorsese watching the dailies. Like a defensive coordinator breaking tape from a football game, drawing x's and arrows to tighten choreography and see what worked.

A musical might be an obvious angle—so many places for songs about the day's routine. Maybe a Gershwin vibe? I had a terrible singing voice, but I could write some lyrics. We could get a team in. The mommy consumer industry was huge; Kickstarter was a thing. There was space for this; it was just a matter of getting it out into the world!

Things clicked along as the weeks went by. Jackson was doing well; Rachel and Keith were pleased. We still hadn't acknowledged the camera. I knew why. Talking about it was like ruining a good date by constantly saying aloud, "This is so fun!" It would mess with the good thing we had going.

Five months into the job, I broke the news to Rachel that I was moving to a different city. One day not long after, she was home early from work, and we had tea together at the kitchen table while Jackson napped. Rachel talked about finding my replacement.

"There's so many things to think about!" she exclaimed, hand to her head. "It worked out great with you, but it's so worrying to bring in a new person. To trust someone in your home! Before you started, all my friends told me to get a nanny cam."

The forbidden subject, out in the open. I put down my tea mug. Finally, accolades for my hard work, but also—an acknowledgement of how entertaining I was. My own Oscar ceremony, right here. I prepared my humblest expression.

"Yeah," Rachel continued. "I even thought about putting one in."

Huh?

"Oh," I said. "I thought you did put one in." I kept my voice bright. "Since you asked about it at the interview."

Rachel put down her mug and looked at me, "No, I never ended up doing it. Wait—did you think there were cameras in here?"

She burst out laughing. "That's so funny!"

I smiled back at her.

Frigging frig! Frigging, frigging, frigging FRIG!

As we approached my leaving date, I was burnt out. I allowed myself not only to be imperfect, but lazy. Keep Jackson happy and nothing extra. I'm not wiping the kitchen counter ten times a day. I'm NOT.

They had hired someone who was going to overlap with me for a few days before I left. The day before the new nanny joined, Rachel updated me on the sleep training they were starting with Jackson. "Let him cry for five minutes before you go in and get him," she told me.

It was my last day alone. At nap time, I put Jackson down in his room and watched from the kitchen on the baby monitor as he stood in his crib and hollered. We hit five minutes. I decided I would see how he did if I let him go a little longer. I bet he would tire himself out soon.

We hit seven minutes. Jackson was still yelling. My cell phone lit up: Keith. He sounded frantic. He said Jackson had been crying more than five minutes and they were following the sleep training strictly and we weren't supposed to let him cry more than five and could I please go get him?

He told me he had seen everything on the nanny camera that they had just put in for the new nanny.

I wish they hadn't waited until Season Two to start watching. Because Season One was fantastic.

Acknowledgements

Many thanks to Alissa Weiss, Adam Wodka, Neil Bardhan, and of course, Jeff Martin. Thanks also to all the wonderful readers of the YO newsletter. Talk soon.

Irish Goodbye